CANOE POLING

"Standing tall and carrying the big stick"

By Harry Rock

Published by Little Dancer

Published by Little Dancer Ltd
61, Benthal Road
London N16 7AR

ISBN: 978-0-9551537-0-9
0-9551537-0-0

Printed in the UK

Dedication

To my wife Anne who has supported my involvement and passion for canoe poling and who has been an active supporter of the poling community.

CONTENTS

INTRODUCTION

Welcome to the world of canoe poling. This is an exciting opportunity to "stand tall and carry a big stick" by using your canoe in ways that have long been forbidden, primarily that of standing upright in an open canoe.

Throughout our childhood training, we were always instructed to never stand up in a canoe, because we were told that it is a very tipsy craft, possibly resulting in the "unpremeditated spill". However, nothing could be more removed from the truth. After proper body positioning and 60 seconds of balance exercises, you will be surprised at how stable you really are while standing, in many cases even more stable than most paddlers who are sitting.

The second rule we break is that we spend most of our time going upstream against the relentless current instead of downstream.

Poling is often referred to as the ultimate low water canoe sport as it is best utilized when the rivers are too shallow for paddling. As summer river levels fall and most canoes are put away to collect dust, poling extends the boating season. Canoes require a very shallow draft, but low water conditions do not allow for the proper use of the paddle, generally resulting in having to push off the bottom and ruining the end of a beautiful blade.

With a pole, you are now able to explore channels and sections of rivers that are not normally accessible during high water conditions. The pole allows you the fun and challenge of negotiating complex rock gardens, climbing drops and ledges that disappear during high water conditions.

Poling is essentially nothing more than an application of angle and leverage. Angle defines the position of the canoe to the current as well as the position of the pole relative to the river bottom. Leverage determines propulsion based on the angle of the pole to the bottom of the river and the amount of force the poler is able to exert on the pole. If canoe angle and pole angle are properly set, there are few ledges, drops, or upstream climbs that can't be attained based on the leverage you are able to obtain off the bottom.

But why pole? Many canoeists ask.

Poling effectively rules out the need for car shuttles as the put in and the takeout are one and the same. It means that you can take your canoe with you and drop it in at any river crossing you see.

A word of caution however is the fact that it takes about twice as long to move against the current as it does to move with it, so be aware of how far you have poled downstream before deciding to turn around and come back upstream.

It allows a person to get on the river before or after work for an hour of fun during the week when most other boaters are only using their canoes on the weekends.

The greatest benefit of poling is the quiet and solitude one has by being on the river by yourself, not dependant on anyone else, thus allowing you to escape the stress and pressures of everyday life. There is nothing better than being on the river at sunrise in the summer when there is a mist on the water, with animals coming down for drinks of water while listening to the orchestra of birds singing to each other.

Early morning poling during the week is a terrific way to start the day. In the evening the beavers are active, swimming or pulling branches underwater to their lodges as you glide by. Watch the fish and turtles swimming by. So take advantage of requiring no car shuttles, and use the river when you chose, not when you are dependant on finding a partner to set up the shuttle. Use it as a means of gaining access to those pristine streams and lakes for camping and fishing that you can't normally reach due to a lack of roads. Escape to your favorite area of wilderness, grab your pole and enjoy pushing the big stick while making that canoe dance in the rapids. Carry your camping gear, climb the river to that wonderful wilderness setting, and enjoy the challenge of successfully negotiating everything the river has to throw at you with its relentless current and rapids.

1: HISTORY OF POLING

The pole is certainly looked at as being the grandfather of the paddle. Early man, when confronted with how to cross or navigate rivers, would naturally have found logs to float on and then used a long stick to push off the bottom for propulsion. Eventually as people became more sophisticated, the dugout canoe evolved and they found that shortening the stick and flattening one end created the paddle, as we know it today.

Many historical paintings and drawings depict the use of the pole going back hundreds of years, especially throughout Mexico and Central America where it was used to help with fishing and transportation.

The pole has continued to play a part in the history of the canoe. Prior to the American Revolutionary War, future American President George Washington had a river freighting company which would move freight from the Ohio River valley down the Potomac River to Georgetown which was a major shipping port. They built log rafts to carry cargo and then poled down the Potomac River. Once in port, they would either sell the rafts as firewood or pole back upstream.

During the American Revolution, George Washington's famous Christmas Eve crossing of the Delaware River at the battle of Trenton was done with large boats using poles to push across to the opposite shore.

In September 1775 Benedict Arnold's plan to capture Fort Quebec was approved by George Washington to prevent the British from invading the Colonies from the north out of Canada. The plan was to sail from Newburyport, Massachusetts with 1,100 troops up the coast to the Kennebec River and then pole up to the Dead River to the Chaudiere and on to Fort Quebec. They left in September with food for 45 days and picked up 200 double-ended overgrown dories called Bateaux that weighed 400 pounds each.

Unfortunately, the Bateaux were purchased from carpenters who used green lumber and the boats leaked continuously. The barrels of bread, dried cod and dried peas burst through the seams as they absorbed water, ruining many of their supplies. They had planned to fish on the way up, but an unexpected hurricane flooded the river and ruined the fishing. They fell behind schedule and were physically worn down as they struggled up the Kennebec fighting the rapids. By the time this rag tag army reached Fort Quebec on New Year's Eve, they were hungry and poorly supplied. The reinforcing American army from the south had turned back with badly needed supplies and Arnold's men were soundly beaten and sent retreating back to the Colonies.

In the late 1700's and early 1800's, the beaver fur trade took off, as beaver hats became the rage in England. Enterprises such as the Hudson Bay Fur Trading Company, Northwest Fur Trading Company and the American Fur Trading Company came into existence to take full advantage of the opportunity to cash in on this trendy fashion. Time was of the essence for these businesses, as they had to gain access into the rich beaver country of the North American interior wilderness before the rivers froze over. Voyageurs would leave Thunder Bay on Lake Superior in late August and paddle upstream with their winter supplies. When confronted with sections of rapids, they would either portage around or use a combination of lining and poling. Early on, the portage trails were poor to non-existent. This is where the birch bark canoes took their worst beating, as limbs and sticks would puncture the fragile birch bark skin. It also took time to move cargo around rapids due to having to make multiple portage trips. It was far more efficient and time saving to use lines to help control the bow of the canoe and pull the canoe upstream as the canoe men used poles to push. The race against the calendar was critical in order to get to their desired trapping grounds prior to winter setting in. They then had the same race to get out by early summer to greet the ships leaving for England. Any delay would make months of trapping worthless if they missed the ships.

Use of the pole in third world countries is still prevalent as is evident from the many pictures that are common showing

9

people moving along waterways in canoes and boats using long poles to push off the bottom. It has had its place with the gondolas of Venice and the junks of China. In today's world, the most notable use of the pole is with the Maine guides who have for decades used it to move their "sporties" or clients into the pristine fishing and hunting grounds by using the remote waterways to move upstream into the wilderness areas.

Jim Conners, a river guide on the St. John River during the 1930s and 40s, recalled that the guides were very competitive about who could pole a canoe the fastest. They would sit around the fire at night, telling stories comparing how fast they were. One way to lay claim to being really quick with the pole was to say that the holes you left in the water didn't even have time to close before you had moved on. Tom Gardner said once that he came up through the rapids so fast there was a row of holes (in the river) where he put that pole. The holes were in the water and drifting back through the rapids. He would turn to another guide and say, "I don't suppose you believe me, do you?" And the other guide would say, "The hell I don't. I came up behind you and I used the same holes." *From the Archives of Maine Folklife Center at the University of Maine, Orono.*

Poling was recognized as a USA national canoeing discipline in 1965 by the American Canoe Association. This was through the efforts of the Beletz brothers, Syl, Al and Frank, of Maplewood, Missouri, who authored the first book on poling, "Canoe Poling". *Published by A.C.Mackenzie Press, 1974.* Al was the USA national chairman of poling for the ACA for 14 years. The brothers were the ones who started the competitive aspect of poling by introducing the first US National Canoe Poling Championships in 1965 at Times Beach on the Meramec River. Until that time the pole was always a shaved down wooden sapling made of ash or spruce. It was, and still is, usually finished off with a steel shoe, or a small sleeve of brass or aluminum at one end to prevent it from splitting as only one end is used. It was the Beletz brothers who revolutionized the sport by introducing the first aluminum pole which was light, stiff and able to be flipped over to utilize both ends, resulting in more efficiency, higher speed and more maneuverability.

Since then the pole hasn't changed much other than the end

plugs and spikes. In 1977 the national competition moved from the Midwest to the East Coast, landing in North Carolina on the Nantahala River. In 1979 it came to Connecticut and has remained in the northeast ever since, taking the sport to a new level with technique, equipment and materials. The intensity of the competition has refined the skills to a high degree, challenging the designs of canoes to match the needs of the modern day poler.

Today we see canoes specifically designed for poling using the lightest and strongest materials possible in order to allow the canoe to dance and play in the waves while traversing and negotiating complex rock gardens and rapids, both upstream and down. Edward Hayden of Waterford, Connecticut has been the premier canoe designer when it comes to building a canoe specifically addressing the needs of the poler. Ed uses Kevlar for lightness and designs a nonsymmetrical hull design so the poler can stand at the widest point in the canoe, just behind the center thwart. He has created several models and it has certainly been the canoe of choice over using stock model designs of the mainstream canoe manufacturers.

Never before have we seen the level of difficulty of water attained such as mastering runs up Tariffville Gorge in Connecticut, Zoar Gap in Massachusetts, Railroad Rapids in New York or Power Line Rapids in Wisconsin.

Poling in Great Britain has seen much success and popularity for a country that has limited access to its rivers. Poling is well suited for that country because of its lack of access to long sections of river, being able to start and stop at the same point is very important to a country with small rivers and limited access..

Today's polers have added to the legacy and lessons learned from the polers of years past, taking their abilities, building on them, refining their skills and transforming a formerly utilitarian form of transportation into a fun and delightful day of canoe play on the river with a big stick.

For the modern day poler, it's not about where they are going but how they are getting there and what happens on the way. It's about using responsive lightweight canoes and poles to create a freedom of dancing in the rapids. Nothing is more fun than discovering a challenging set of rapids and spending hours

Canoe Poling

trying to master every combination of moves that include ferries, eddy turns, peal outs, spins, reverse moves and climbing drops while dazzling the crowds with "Rock Hops" and "Rock-a-Copters". Making the canoe go where you want, being able to climb every drop and moving upstream at will against that relentless current is what creates the magic of canoe poling. It is truly taking the river on, taming the current and tapping its energy to allow you to go where you want in an upstream direction.

Could this have been the worlds first poler?

2. GETTING STARTED

The single largest limiting factor in the development and expansion of canoe poling as a discipline has been the lack of adequate poles. There are very few commercial manufacturers and the ones who exist have difficulty in shipping single piece poles due to their length. Most sources of poles have been from resourceful polers who have been able to acquire aluminum stock and manufacture end plugs in their basement and garage shops. Most poles are transported by friends and acquaintances who have purchased a supply of poles when available and then sell them at races and instructional clinics. The small number of polers versus paddlers will never make the commercial aspect of building poles attractive, as we simply can't purchase enough of them to make it worthwhile to manufacture them in bulk. Therefore it is incumbent upon the enthusiast to find those individuals whose hobby it is to build things and put them to work building poles that can then be driven around to individual canoeing events for distribution.

Pole Materials:

Fiberglass and carbon fiber:

Has been experimented with but it has not proven to be durable, especially in the glacial boulder strewn rivers of the Northeast. The problem is the lack of lateral strength in the sidewalls once they are pinched between rocks. When the pole makes contact with the river bottom, its vertical angle changes as the canoe moves forward, thus collapsing the sidewall as the pole is forced with pressure against rocks and boulders.

The other disadvantage of synthetic poles is their flexibility. As power and force are applied, the pole bends tremendously. This creates a major control problem for the boater while moving against the current upstream because the canoe will drift sideways, away from the desired path of travel until the pole begins to spring back. It is very difficult to gain any upstream advantage on stiff current because of all of the polers energy being absorbed by the bending pole rather than being transferred to the river bottom for leverage. Frustration will grow due to not being able to place the canoe where one wants it due to the delay in response and the absorption of energy.

The pole must be plugged with some type of material to allow it to float when it is dropped and to protect the fragile synthetic material from the wear and tear of the rocky bottom.

Its greatest advantage is that it does not pin itself against the side of rocks like aluminum because of a low coefficient of friction. It does slip off rocks however when being used for leverage in turns and spins.

Wood:

Has long been the traditional material of choice to build a pole. River guides have over the generations simply cut or found a suitable thicket of Spruce and cut down a straight sapling to length (10 - 12 feet in length) stripping the bark off after it has dried to prevent it from splitting. Spruce has been the wood of choice because it is lighter and stiffer, although weaker than the heavier alternative of Ash.

The less adventurous of us can find wooden Ash stock at a local lumberyard and then shave it down. Some river outfitters carry commercially manufactured wood poles although they are not very common. The other alternative is to purchase a closet pole. The down side is that closet pole has a great deal of flex, is weak and is not a good selection for long term use.

It is important to ensure that wooden poles are splinter free. The wooden end will also split apart if a steel shoe or brass sleeve is not fitted on the end to absorb impact and wear as the pole is planted on the rocky bottom. A lag bolt can be screwed into the end for improved grip and to protect the wooden end. The wood can be left natural or coated with a varnish finish.

The biggest disadvantage to using a wood pole is its weight. It is much heavier than using an aluminum or synthetic pole and can become very tiring after extended use. It also does not generally allow for double-ended use unless it has been tapered at both ends.

The advantages are that the bottom plants on a rocky bottom are very quiet compared to the clunking of aluminum and it is very warm and comfortable to use during cold water use.

Aluminum :

Has proven to the top choice by most contemporary polers and racers. This has revolutionized the sport of big sticking because of its lightweight and double-ended capability. The light weight makes it very responsive for use from side to side and doesn't cause one to tire quickly. It is very strong and durable. It has flex, yet is stiff enough for total power delivery. It can be straightened out if it has become bent from use so long as the sidewall isn't crimped which may cause it to snap upon re-straightening.

The best way to straighten a bent pole is to find two trees close together and insert the pole between them. With gentle leverage, you can bend the pole back into alignment by pushing the kink against the outer tree and working your way up the damaged section, continuing a series of times until you have it back to normal. If the sidewall is crimped, it will snap off so the best thing is to then use a hacksaw, cut a fresh end, remove the plug from the broken end and reinsert it. You now have a fully useable pole again, albeit a bit shorter. The shorter pole is actually preferred now in racing because it is more responsive, being lighter and quicker to whip around except when you are in deep water conditions.

The disadvantages are that it is cold to hold in chilly water and it is noisy as it makes contact with the bottom. Aluminum must be plugged or it will sink. The choices are wooden dowels, cork, solid aluminum, or a solid synthetic such as Delran. Steel spikes are usually inserted into wood or Delran to assist with grip in ledge conditions and to reduce wear on the plug. Plug outside diameters must be flush with the outside aluminum wall to prevent pinning due to an extended lip.

Aluminum is usually 6061 T6 aircraft tubing with diameter

choices of 1", 1 1/8", or 1 1/4". The larger the diameter, the stronger the pole and less flex it has which is desirable for transferring all of the polers power and energy to pushing off the river bottom directly.

Diameter size may be dictated by hand comfort and how much speed is desired in deep water conditions when using the kayak stroke for propulsion. The most prevalent choice among racers and recreational polers has been the 1 1/8" diameter with a wall thickness of .058" at a standard length of 12 feet. This setup allows for light weight, stiffness, comfort and quickness.

Aluminum must be prepared before use because your grip will tend to slip on the smooth metal. This is accomplished by either roughing up the surface with a file, taping the pole with plastic tape like a candy cane, or by rubbing paraffin or bees wax over the entire length of the pole. This is similar to how surfers apply wax to their surfboards for traction. If using a file, make sure that you rub down the surface afterward with a rag to remove any metal shavings or burrs.

My preference for grip however is a taped pole. It provides enough traction so you are always ensured to have a good grip that won't slip, even if your hands are sweaty. The one caution is that in time, the ribbed surface of the tape will make your hands very sore as the pole moves repeatedly through your hands due to your skin being so soft from being wet. It is also very important to never rub your brow with your hands, as the body oil will transfer to the pole, making it very slippery. I generally always wear thin cotton gardening gloves with little rubber dots on the grip to save on the wear and tear of my hands and to help enhance my grip. Rubber work gloves also work very well for protecting the hands, providing warmth during cold water poling, and improved grip. There is nothing more frustrating than to have applied force on the pole to begin a forward power plant and then have your hands slip, resulting in no forward momentum while still expending the energy.

Footwear:

Proper footwear is critical to maintaining balance and delivering effective power plants. Tremendous thrust and leverage is generated during each power plant that must be transferred to the canoe through the feet. A patterned rubber sole is required to prevent slippage. There are plenty of river sandals, shoes and booties that provide a good platform to stand on. It is important that they are snug so that your feet don't move inside your footwear as you apply leverage to the bottom of the canoe. Footwear should be cleaned before entering the boat to maintain a good surface to stand on. Dirt and sand can act as small roller bearings when force is applied to the contact point between feet and hull.

Canoe Selection:

Part of the appeal of canoe poling is the ability to use any type of recreational canoe, regardless of length, material or width. However, the best overall boat for tracking ability and maneuverability is a standard recreational 16 foot ABS Royalex canoe.

The longer the canoe, the better it tracks and generally the faster it is due to displacing less water. It will float higher and be more stable. The shorter the hull, the more maneuverable it is but it generally will have less glide and it will be tougher to track upstream.

A full hull design at the ends is desired to reduce the porpoising effect from power plants along with a 15 inch center depth to shed waves. A 35-36 inch beam is the recommended width for overall balance and stability. A narrower beam can be used but it will create a less stable craft to stand in although it will generally be a fast canoe running straight up the river.

In heavy water, you want a wider beam to ensure the maximum amount of balance possible. Canoes that immediately taper to the stern from the center thwart tend to sink in the stern when power is being delivered.

ABS is preferred because of its ability to slide off rocks and absorb punishment. However, most of the racing crowd now only uses Kevlar canoes due to the lightweight acceleration and responsiveness that you have in a well-designed boat.

Limited rocker is helpful for turning and maneuverability without causing a loss of tracking ability. Too much rocker will cause the boat to be very difficult to control, resulting in the loss of bow control.

A shallow 'V' hull design helps with tracking and provides good initial and secondary stability because of having a 'shoulder' to stand on versus a flat bottom hull. However, a flat bottomed hull will spin very easily with limited drag or resistance.

Trim:

Canoe trim is critical for successful upstream movement. The boat must be slightly stern heavy to lift the bow stem out of the approaching water. This keeps it from grabbing, tracking and pulling the craft off course into a wild uncontrolled ferry towards shore as you move upstream. The bow must be high enough to allow the current to slide under the hull. Pushing the bow into current creates very difficult control problems. As the gradient steepens and as current increases, the more the bow must be lifted clear of the rushing water. Climbing drops will sometimes dictate moving further back in the hull to create even higher lift to help break over the lip of the ledge.

Downstream travel requires flattening the trim of the canoe by moving closer to the center thwart to increase the wetted surface area for additional speed as long as the boat has reached or exceeded current velocity. The hull now parts water and planes rather than pushing up waves like a powerboat at half speed.

If the canoe is moving slower than the current, then trim must be adjusted so that the stern (upriver end) is higher than the bow (downstream end). This again is necessary to allow water to slide under the hull as the craft moves slowly downstream to keep the upstream end from tracking as the water catches up to the hull. The boater should be in front of the center thwart to create the bow heavy trim. The quickest and most secure way of changing body position in the canoe is by using small hops either forward or backwards. Trying to move each individual foot will cause the boat to rock violently sideways causing a possible upset. To change positions from one side of the thwart to the other you can either cross by walking the center line for stability, or bend over and place the pole in front of the thwart on the gunwales. Then with your center of gravity lowered and your weight stabilized, simply step over the thwart into your new position.

You can always try a "Rock Hop" by jumping over the center thwart landing on the other side. Balance and care must be preserved to ensure a secure landing. This move is a great crowd pleaser but must be practiced for safety and security in landing!

However, I rarely ever move to the other side of the thwart, as I am usually moving as fast as the current unless I am in a highly complex rock garden with difficult moves to make. Generally if you have good control skills, you can hold the upstream stern in place even if it is tending to track, but it does take practice.

Where polers stand in the canoe has a tremendous impact on the amount of speed and glide that is generated. Ideally, the canoe should be evenly trimmed with both ends drafting the same depth of water. The canoe can use its full length for maximum water displacement that results in higher speed and longer glide between power plants. Hull speed increases as the waterline length increases. Therefore, if a 16 foot craft is weighted in the stern resulting in a waterline length of 14 feet, it will be slower than an identical craft that is properly trimmed with a full wetted surface area of 16 feet. The higher the bow, the more it resembles a power boat at slow speed plowing water and pushing a large bow wave creating increased water resistance and slower speed.

Because the dynamics of the power plant causes some down force on the hull, the rear half of the canoe must have a full shape before tapering to the stern to combat the sinking effect which reduces speed and glide. The bow tends to be pushed upward creating a wave for increased resistance. A fuller shape increases the wetted surface area displacement so that the canoe has more of a tendency to plane across the water rather than sinking and creating a stern rooster tail.

Safety Items:

A personal floatation device (PFD) should always be worn

regardless of the depth and difficulty of the water. The best choice is a type III over the shoulder vest because it offers floatation around the entire torso area. It provides warmth and protection against the elements and padding against rocks when taking those unplanned swims through the rapids as you scrape across the rocks.

Helmets are recommended to protect the head in case of sudden exits from the boat due to pole pins, missed pole plants and unexpected stops after impacting large rocks. I have had pinned poles spring back and hit me soundly in the head as I worked to free them after being jammed between rocks. I also came close to losing an eye and injuring my head after falling out of the canoe against a rock when a pole plant slipped as I was climbing a difficult drop. While injuries are rare, they do occur, so always err on the side of safety.

3: FORWARD PROPULSION

Classic Style Stance:

The classic style stance is what the power poling stance evolved from. It was used to pole loaded 18 and 20 foot canoes upstream where the poler was standing closer to the end of the canoe where it narrows down. This required offsetting the person's feet because of the reduced width of the canoe as it tapers to the end. (Fig 2)

The poler would lean the forward leg into the rear thwart or seat and the rear leg would brace against the gunwale. This style was very effective for helping to snub down a tricky section of rapids by providing good leverage and a solid stance with which to try to slow or stop the weighted canoe while descending a section of river.

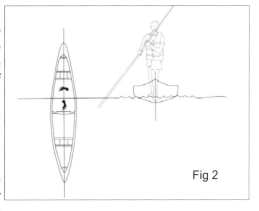

Fig 2

The classic style uses a diagonal stance with the offside foot placed in front of the onside foot, against the opposite chine of the canoe for balance. This sets the polers body at a diagonal angle to the midline of the canoe, thereby forcing the poler to only pole on one side of the canoe.

The diagonal stance does provide greater power and leverage for the poler but it restricts switching sides without resetting one's feet. This style is effective for straight line travel in pushing a heavy canoe but is not useful for technical maneuvering or dancing in the rapids requiring quick changes from side to side.

Power Poling Stance:

The "power poling stance" is the body position that has revolutionized freestyle poling and separated it from "classic style poling" which uses the diagonal stance. Almost all competitors incorporate the squared off stance which allows the poler to work both sides of the canoe with ease. (Fig 3& Plates 2/3/4) The poler should stand one to two feet behind the center thwart. The person's personal weight determines how far to stand behind the thwart in order to create a slightly stern heavy trim which helps with bow control when moving upstream. The feet should be spread as wide as possible, positioned under the shoulders and up against the chine's of the canoe. Body position should be perpendicular to the midline of the canoe. This wide stance provides tremendous control and balance as the boat pitches and rolls through the waves. Keep your knees slightly bent

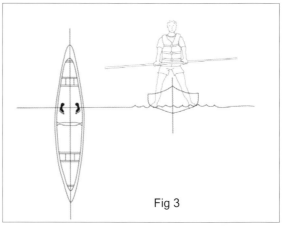

Fig 3

to act as shock absorbers with a slight forward lean of 10 to 15 degrees at the waist to enhance balance and leverage. Don't stand stiffly or just bend at the knees.

You need to have forward body lean to reach as high on the angled pole as possible and to keep your center of gravity lower for stability. It also allows you to incorporate a higher degree of leverage on the pole by having a more aggressive body position so that you can lean against the pole as you start to load it with power.

The biggest problem beginners have is developing balance. The following exercise is good for establishing balance and confidence in your stance. (Fig 4 & Plate 1)

- Establish your stance and proper body position in the canoe.
- Grip the pole like a kayak paddle and hold it waist high as if a tightrope walker holding a balance bar.
- Slowly start weighting and un-weighting each leg by bending one knee and then the other to create a rocking motion in the canoe. As the canoe rolls from side to side, the heel of your un-weighted foot should lift up off the hull at the top of the roll while maintaining contact with the hull with the balls of your feet. All motion should come from the waist down; the upper body should be quiet and practically stationary. This motion is very similar to the weighting and un-weighting of the inside leg in downhill skiing.
- Speed up the rocking motion until each gunwale touches the water, emphasizing control.
- Then try just weighting one leg and allowing the gunwale to come close to touching the water without taking water over the rail. This helps to build balance and boat control with each foot.

Fig 4

Practice this exercise each time you get on the water so the canoe starts to feel like an extension of your body. Remember that your feet should never move relative to the bottom of the canoe during this exercise. In time you should be able to weight one side of the canoe and lift the un-weighted foot completely off the hull while standing stationary on the other foot.

With practice and improved balance, this move will always be a good crowd pleaser, displaying boat control with the water kissing the gunwale while waving your un-weighted foot at them.

Power Delivery:

To generate forward propulsion, one must understand the mechanics of the power plant that is the primary source of straight line movement in a canoe using a pole.

Like paddling, unless proper technique is applied, canoe speed and direction will be misdirected and slow.

Study and concentration of proper execution and technique will result in an efficient use of energy transforming into top speed and distance traveled.

Boaters need to be selfish when it comes to conserving energy while achieving maximum results. This helps accomplish established goals whether it is winning races or just enjoying a cruise on a river.

This lesson is pointed out only too well from watching world class athletes who make things look so easy with little apparent effort. Their technique is both highly refined and efficient resulting in a high degree of finesse. It is this finesse that makes them the best in their discipline, achieving maximum results with minimum output. They exude efficiency while minimizing energy expenditures.

Power Plant Techniques:

The power poling style has revolutionized the sport of poling. This style is most commonly equated with what racers use in competition. Canadian canoe legend Bill Mason, after watching me with fascination a number of years ago at the LL Bean sponsored Maine Canoe Symposium, compared it to freestyle paddling by taking a traditional discipline and bringing it to another level with unlimited control and moves with no restraints. What was once thought of as just a "grunt and grind" means of pushing upriver is now fun, challenging and exciting. We actually look forward to going out "to push the big stick".

The transformation of this esoteric, little known form of canoe sport into something that has gained national recognition as a respected discipline has to do with the stance. By squaring off the traditional diagonal stance into the power poling stance of today, an entirely new poling arena has opened up for accomplishing river maneuvers and skills. To understand power poling, one must study its makeup including handgrip, pole angle, leverage, and power delivery.

Hand Grip:

In canoe poling there are two prominent grips. The first is the batters grip (Fig 5) that is only used for delivering power. The name comes from how a person grips a baseball bat with the

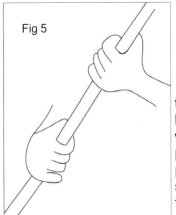

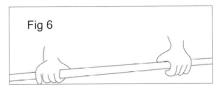

Fig 5

Fig 6

thumbs on top. The second is a kayak grip (Fig 6) that is only utilized when using a kayak motion with the pole in deep water or on griping the pole when incorporating corrective strokes to change or adjust the forward direction of the canoe. This grip requires the thumbs facing each other. So quickly put, thumbs on top for power, thumbs together when correcting direction.

On Side/Off Side:

On side/off side refers to the side of the canoe that the pole is positioned at that given time. If the pole is on the boater's port side, then the left side is the onside and the right side is the offside. If the pole switches sides, then the canoeist's starboard side becomes the onside and the left side is the off side.

Pole Angle:

This aspect has a major impact on the effectiveness of power poling. For forward movement, the bottom of the pole must always be planted just behind the poler, resulting in a forward angle of the pole. Ideally the pole should be about 45 degrees. (Fig 7)

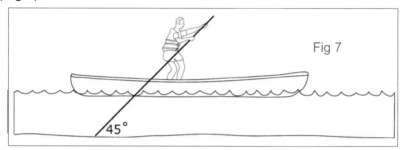

Fig 7

45°

Too often beginners plant the pole in front of their body and try to pull the canoe past the pole. This position creates very poor leverage because there is nothing to pull against and the pole has no weight on it to keep it in place. The pole is also in a vertical position that tends to create all upward force rather than forward motion on the canoe. The body is pulled forward and off balance because there is no way to stabilize it against the pulling motion.

Leverage:

With proper pole angle, effective leverage can be applied. Because the desired result is forward motion, the ideal situation would be a wall placed behind the canoe after each glide phase so that the pole could be planted against it in a horizontal position. This would create total forward force on the canoe for 100% efficiency.

Unfortunately, this is not possible so a compromise of a 45-degree angle is made by planting the pole on the bottom. As a result, two forces are created as power is applied on the pole. In a weightless environment, theoretically the canoe would jettison into the air at a 45-degree angle to the water surface because of the generated force. Because gravity negates this affect, two things happen to the canoe. First, the stern tends to sink because of the down force on the hull which is why a fuller hull design is important. Second, as the canoe reacts to the applied force, it moves forward.

Leverage and pole angle are closely aligned to each other. If the pole angle is greater than 45 degrees, more up force is created than forward motion. This creates a porpoising effect on the hull as the stern is pushed down and then pops back up when the pressure is released. If the pole angle is less than 45 degrees, less down force is created on the hull and more forward force is generated, which is desirable. However the pole tends to slip out because there is less down force to hold it in place. The pole which is buoyant wants to float upward. Sometimes when passing large boulders, you can actually plant the pole against the dry portion of the rock to gain pure straight line power.

Power Delivery:

Once the pole has been planted with proper angle, you are ready to deliver power.

- Both hands should be placed as high as you can on the pole with thumbs on top in a batters grip to maximize the range of motion once the power phase is initiated. The hands will usually be spread apart by several inches.
- The knees should be bent.
- The offside hand should be on top of the onside (pole) hand. As force is applied, the large back muscles should be used to pull the hands past the hip before starting the recovery phase for the next plant.
- Once the leverage motion begins, proper pole angle is necessary to maintain bottom purchase and keep the pole plant from slipping.
- After acceleration is underway, the force on the pole diminishes somewhat reducing the amount of down force required to hold it in place.

Now the poler can concentrate on forward force production. As a result, he/she can begin sinking the body and bending at the knees and leaning against the pole. This can be compared to leaning against the wall with your legs in a sitting position without a chair. The forward pull on the pole keeps the body from falling over backwards. The sinking motion helps to reduce the pole angle relative to the water surface to generate more forward force and less up/down force on the canoe. Sinking of the body also helps maintain balance. The more forward force that is generated, the more the body must lean back against the pole in order to transfer the force through the body to the feet which are essentially pushing the canoe upstream.

Hand Over Hand Technique:

This technique is very effective for climbing steep drops, moving against strong current and for people who don't have strong upper bodies.

Simply plant the pole behind you at a 45 degree angle and start climbing the pole by reaching up as high as you can with each hand and pulling back towards yourself, one over the other

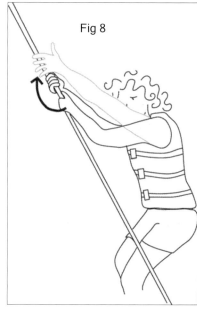

Fig 8

until you reach the end of the pole. (Fig 8 & Plate 5)

Understand that you are essentially pulling the canoe past the pole's point of purchase on the river bottom. This motion is similar to climbing a steep hill with a guide rope in place where you use your hands to help climb up the hill by pulling on the rope, hand over hand.

Bend your knees and lean away from the bow for leverage to help push the canoe forward by transferring the force generated from your hands through your feet to the canoe.

This hand over hand motion is often described as looking similar to what children do with a baseball bat when picking sides for baseball or softball game. For additional power, finish off the motion once you reach the top end of the pole with a power plant using a final thrust.

Pole Recovery:

Quick and rapid pole recovery after each power plant is very important when traveling upstream. The longer the pole is off the bottom, the more momentum you will lose, particularly when you're climbing drops and fighting accelerating water being funneled into a chute. Minimum recovery time is of the essence for maximum power delivery in order to make constant headway against the current. All three of the following recoveries can be used with either power plants or hand over hand climbing techniques.

Pool Cue:

This is the fastest and most efficient method for pole recovery when climbing upstream.

- At the end of either a power plant or a hand over hand climb, form a circle around the pole with the thumb and forefinger of your onside hand, similar to the one used by pool players, with the hand positioned by your hip.
- Then quickly thrust the pole upward with your offside hand which starts out on top of your onside hand to send the pole sliding forward and up through the pool cue hand which remains next to your hip. The end of the pole should exit the water and pass just inches over it to reduce drag through the water.
- Once the pole is fully returned, bring the lower hand quickly up to meet the offside thrusting hand which is already as high as possible and let gravity return the pole to the bottom by releasing your grip and allowing the pole to drop. This should be a very fluid motion which requires practice to master.
- The pole will fall nearly vertical but the forward motion of the canoe will return it to a 45-degree angle just as

you start to load it with force again for the next power plant.

In particularly fast flow, you may actually have to force the pole down into position to gain purchase on the bottom, as the current will be trying to sweep the end of the pole downstream.

Windmill Recovery:

This technique is very effective on flatwater or easy upstream and downstream sections. After power is applied, the pole is simply flipped end-over-end like a windmill (Fig 9 & Plates 6/7/8) so that the wet end becomes the dry end and vice versa after each power plant.

Fig 9

This generates more power plants per minute than any other recovery technique, resulting in greater speed. The pole always remains on one side of the canoe during this recovery which requires the poler to be able to control the bow without having to change sides.

The disadvantage with the windmill recovery is that the pole reenters the water vertically when you're moving downstream and it tends to pin or jam between rocks as your entry angle and exit angle are sharply different. As a result you may need to let it go (down the creek without a pole) or risk bending the pole or being catapulted out of the back of the canoe, all of which has happened to me.

When moving upstream with this technique, you can't gain effective leverage off the bottom because there is no forward angle on the pole once it is planted. This is caused by resistance on the hull which limits forward glide because of the opposing current. Because the canoe does not glide past the pole once it is planted you are left with a forward pole angle of 70 or 80 degrees which is too steep, rather than the optimal 45 degrees assuming that the water is 0 degrees.

This is the easiest recovery for beginners to learn. The biggest problem newcomers have is in keeping the canoe moving in a straight line.

Follow these steps:

- After you've completed the power plant, release the onside hand, which is now by your hip, and turn it over with your palm up.
- Reach down and re-grip the lower half of the pole about one foot below your original grip with the onside hand so that the thumb is facing the water.
- Rotate or swing the wet end up and over (counter clockwise) with the onside hand while using the offside hand as the point of rotation by your hip and direct the dry end towards the water, thus changing contact ends of the pole on the bottom.
- Release the offside hand just as the pole enters the water and re-grip on top of the onside hand (both thumbs are on top in the batters grip).
- Lift your hands as high as possible to reposition for the next plant and loosen your grip so the pole slides through your hands. Begin the next power plant once the pole has regained bottom purchase. You actually start to pull with the onside hand that allows the offside hand to re-grip the pole in a higher position to allow for a longer pole plant.

Crossover Windmill:

This is the same motion as the windmill except the pole alternates the sides of the canoe. This is very effective for climbing stiff current and maintaining a proper bow angle. The motion of crossing over the hull easily sets the pole up with an immediate 45-degree angle in the water ready to provide effective leverage. This is a very effective means of attaining movement on the river as you control the bow with power being delivered on both sides of the canoe alternatively while moving up against a difficult gradient.

The difference between this and the windmill recovery is that the offside hand guides the dry end of the pole down and across the hull into position on the opposite side of the canoe. The onside hand continues bringing the wet end up and into position. The previous offside hand now becomes the onside hand and re-grips the pole below the other hand.

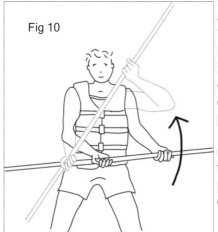

Fig 10

Here is a breakdown of the maneuver step by step. Note that the onside and offside positions will change with each crossover move.

- After you've completed the power plant, release the onside hand and turn it over with the palm up, facing the sky.
- Reach down and re-grip the lower half of the pole so that the thumb is facing the water.
- Rotate and guide the wet end up and over (counter clockwise) with the onside hand while using the offside hand as the point of rotation to direct the dry end towards the water on the opposite side of the canoe. The point of rotation should be in front of the body at mid waist. The offside hand should guide the pole from one side of the body to the other as the pole is making its rotation so that it now becomes the onside hand.
- Release the new onside hand just as the pole enters the water and re-grip below the new offside hand (both thumbs are on top) as the pole is sliding through your relaxed grip on the pole to reach the river bottom. The

hands should be repositioning themselves as high as possible as you prepare for the next power plant. With practice, this should be a very fluid and quick maneuver.

- Begin the next power plant once the pole has regained purchase on the river bottom.
- The pole should be parallel to the midline of the canoe once it is planted so that pure forward force is generated after the pole is loaded with power.

Rudder Action:

Whether you're paddling or poling, the canoe can be a very pesky craft to direct. It doesn't want to move in a straight line and it will try to take the scenic route among the bushes and rocks along the shore. Learning to generate pure forward force will help eliminate unpredicted turns but you'll need to learn how to rudder in the early stages of your poling career until you gain total control of your bow.

Ruddering is a sure way of maintaining a straight course, especially when pushing along on flatwater or mild upstream stretches. Most beginners will find this helpful for maintaining directional control until power plants are mastered, providing pure forward force. At the end of every power plant, simply allow the pole to float up and use it as a rudder for correctional direction by dragging it along straight behind the canoe for two or three seconds. This is usually enough time to have an affect on the bow. If more correction is required, simply move the pole in or out with your lower hand (onside) and the bow will quickly respond in the direction the pole was moved to, either left or right. Then execute the desired pole recovery for the next power plant.

As your technique improves, you'll need to rudder less and less. Understand that ruddering is something that should be used very sparingly as the canoe is rapidly slowing down the longer the pole is in the rudder position as there is no forward force being generated. While you're learning, however, keep these points in mind:

- The slower the canoe is moving, the more the bow will tend to wander, so some forward speed is necessary to keep yourself in a straight line.
- Beginners are often hesitant to put much force in their forward power plants but it is necessary to exert some strength and force to ensure enough hull speed for the rudder action to take effect.
- Too much correction is often worse than not enough. Many novices, upon seeing the bow swing off by five or ten degrees, will counter with 20 or 30 degrees of correction.
- Remember, you only need enough correction to bring the bow back to where it started. It's much like baking a cake; just because the recipe calls for a pinch of salt doesn't mean you add a cupful to make sure you have enough. Just add the right amount to end up with the desired result.

Plate 1
Developing balance: A good drill for developing balance is to stand in the chine of the canoe on one foot. A necessary skill when conducting radical leans whilst performing turns, side slipping, surfing and running through rapids.

Plate 2
Power poling requires the poler to have a squared off stance, knees bent, pole angled forward with the hands grasping the pole above the head about six inches apart. Note the heavy stern trim due to the poler standing about 12 inches behind the centre thwart.

Plate 3
Foot position, Power poling. Note the squared off stance, offering greater versatility by using both sides of the canoe for power plants, a very stable position when poling heavy whitewater.

Plate 4
Classic style poling requires the offside foot to be placed ahead of the onside foot. All the power moves are conducted on the on side of the canoe. This is most effective with loaded canoes.

Plate 5
With the hand over hand technique, the poler continually reaches up, hand over hand pulling the canoe towards the end of the pole before recovering for the next hand over hand pole

Plate 6
The Windmill recovery requires the poler to release the lower (Onside) hand at the end of the power plant and re-grip the pole with the thumb facing down.

Plate 7
The poler rotates the pole over in a forward windmill rotation, changing the dry end with the wet end.

Plate 8
The poler reaches up and re-establishes the power poling position for the next power plant.
Note: the angle of the pole.

Plate 9
The poler starts the forward sweep stroke by positioning the pole in the catch position as far forward and as close to the bow as possible

Plate 10
The poler sweeps the pole in a horizontal position past the 90° point.
Note: the further the point of contact of the pole with the water, the more powerful the turning force on the canoe.

Plate 11
The Poler completes the 180° sweep with the pole touching the stern of the canoe.
Note: The upper body has twisted around with the chest following the pole with both hands extended over the water at the end of the stroke

Plate 12/13
With the reverse sweep the poler positions the pole behind
their body so that the pole is as close to the stern as possible.
The poler then pushes their hip outwards so the pole is able
to be pulled against it creating a powerful point of leverage
with the offside hand pulling against their body. The pole only
rotates to a 90° position before recovering for an additional
reverse sweep if necessary.

4. CONTROLLING YOUR BOW

The mark of the accomplished boater, whether paddler or poler is the ability to control their bow and move the canoe where they choose, not where the river decides to take it.

Nowhere is this more noticeable than poling upstream. The key to successful upstream travel is keeping the bow pointed directly into the oncoming water. As soon as the bow falls off a degree or two, the canoe will begin to ferry and move away from the desired path of travel. Unless a quick correction is made, the angle of error will rapidly grow in magnitude. There are several factors which can be adjusted to keep this from happening.

Trim:

Trim of the boat is a critical item. The canoe must have a stern (downstream end) heavy trim. This keeps the bow (upstream end) stem of the craft from grabbing and tracking off course. The approaching water is able to flow under the bow without issue and you can effectively determine and control your direction. The bow stem should just break out of the water without exposing an extensive amount of hull, which will cause the canoe to have a large amount of upward angle, thus slowing the forward speed while pushing a large bow wake. Boat leans, leg drive and pole leverage are all factors in helping to move the bow around easily as long as the bottom can slide easily without resistance from the bow stem digging in and pushing water laterally.

Power Delivery:

The way power is applied to the canoe will determine how well upstream direction is maintained. You must remember that when power is generated on one side of the hull, the boat will automatically veer to the opposite side. Perfectly executed power plants will minimize this but it is a natural factor to recognize and to deal with.

Polers with advanced technique should be able to pole continuously on one side or the other without needing to apply correction or changing sides. The best compensation other than corrective strokes, which slow the canoe down, is to simply alternate sides using cross over windmill recoveries so power is being delivered evenly. This will automatically correct angle error.

Reading Water:

Knowing how to read water and use it to your advantage is a very important skill to master. Recognizing where the current is coming from will determine how straight a course you will travel.

Looking at the shoreline can be very misleading because the current sometimes moves diagonally across the riverbed. You can determine water direction by watching for bubbles, leaves, sticks and eddy lines. These are all excellent indicators as to the direction that water is moving.

The bow must be pointed directly into the approaching water so there is equal resistance on each side of the hull, causing the boat to move in a straight line.

Pole Plants and Recovery:

The choice of power delivery and pole recoveries will make a difference in how easily you ascend waterways. Essentially there are two options based on position in the river. If you are climbing up the middle of the channel, then power is going to be required on both sides of the hull for automatic course correction by using the cross over windmill recovery for generating alternating power to each side of the canoe.

If you are hugging the shoreline, then a pool cue recovery in conjunction with power plants keeps the power delivery on one side. You can also use a hand over hand climbing technique with the pole being restricted to use between the boat and the shore. This enables the poler to keep the bow tucked in towards the shore if you are going against a very difficult current.

The hand over hand technique allows you to generate significant leverage against the current without expending a high energy consumption. It also allows you to push the stern out if necessary to keep the bow tucked in towards the shore and out of the main flow if it starts to drift out. It is much easier to move the stern in or out than the bow which has constant frontal resistance on it because of the approaching current.

Deciding whether or not to use power pole plants or hand over hand pole plants will be based on the strength of the current and the incline degree of gradient pitch. Power plants are more powerful but they are energy taxing based on the difficulty of the approaching water. The hand over hand climbing technique is slower but easier to execute, especially in steep climbs.

An important factor to keep in mind at all times is that the slower the hull speed, the harder it is to keep the bow in line and the more it wants to drift off course. Recovery time between plants must be kept to a minimum to maximize the number of plants per minute. As soon as the power phase ends and the recovery begins, hull speed drops immediately. The stiffer the current, the faster the canoe will decelerate and the shorter the glide will be. If it falls to less than that of the current, the boat will stall and begin to drift backwards while losing its hull alignment to the current, making correction and recovery very difficult.

5. DEEP WATER TECHNIQUE

People always question how you are able to traverse deep water because of the assumption that the poler must be confined to shallow water when using a 12-foot pole. The answer is that water depth doesn't make any difference.

People are always amazed to see how fast they are able to move through deep water. Whether you are pushing along the lake shore or shallow river sections, sooner or later you have to cross deep water to reach the opposite lake shore or to cross pools separating rapids. Contrary to what most people think, movement of a canoe with a 1 ¼" diameter pole using a modified kayak stroke is quite fast. An efficient solo poler can easily maintain the same pace as a team of paddlers. This appears impossible to most observers due to the lack of paddle blades on the pole, but the key is the amount of leverage the poler is exerting on the water and the number of strokes per minute being executed. Easy cruising with an improved vantage point makes this an interesting alternative to sitting and paddling for many recreational boaters.

Fig 11

I generally start instructional classes with beginners by teaching the kayak stroke (Fig 11) because of the student's ability to learn the technique immediately. This allows them to experience instant success and become excited about learning more about the sport. It is also an easy way to help beginners develop balance.

At first most people will start out stiff legged, maintaining an upright body position and just using their arms while initiating the pole rotation. However, correct technique is necessary to allow for the most efficient and energy conserving style possible. The following section will break down the technique into two components, upper and lower body motion.

Upper Body:

Upper body motion should be very smooth and rhythmical. The pole should enter the water with little splash and limited noise culminating in an even pull and clean exit.

Follow these steps for proper technique.

- Stand in the power poling stance and grip the pole shoulder width or slightly wider, equal distance from the middle. Grip the pole with the kayak grip with your thumbs facing each other.
- Lean forward 15-20 degrees at the waist, with your knees slightly bent to increase balance and leverage.
- Rotate your onside shoulder forward, as you would in a kayak, so that the onside arm can reach well ahead to plant the pole in the catch position where the pole enters the water near the gunwale at the bow of the canoe, before starting to pull and creating leverage.
- Insert the pole two to three feet into the water with the pole as vertical as possible, eliminating any side sweeping action which will create some turning force on the bow of the canoe. There should be a slight bend to the onside elbow with the offside arm being bent and almost horizontal at the catch position (the point at which the pole has entered the water but before power is applied).
- Begin to roll and rotate the upper back at the waist so that there is an uncoiling of the upper torso to ensure that the large back muscles are doing the major work, not the smaller arm muscles.
- Continue the power phase past the hip and then recover into the next power phase by rotating the lower

hand up for a clean exit. The power phase should be a complete pulling motion to the hip, but not a pushing motion past the hip.

- The stroke should pull evenly and in a straight line, parallel to the desired direction of travel and very close to the side of the canoe to prevent any loss of forward power. As the stroke ends, the upper body is immediately prepared for the next stroke (on the other side of the canoe) because the shoulder plane has already rotated forward. The pole should make a ripping noise as it moves through the water without any splash.

Lower Body:

Your legs should constantly move using a weighting and un-weighting motion similar to the bicycling motion you would see in marathon paddling.

As the pole pulls back and the upper hand moves across the frontal plane of the body, the offside leg un-weights slightly and bends a little at the knee.

The onside leg is weighted and pushes down. A rhythmic action results matching up with the upper body motion. This causes the boat to rock slightly from side to side allowing for an extended reach and pole extension into the water during the forward rotation of the upper body. The increased extension is because the onside rail (gunwale) is lower to the water and out of the way of the pole. The leg motion is not very exaggerated.

Practice on flatwater is highly recommended to develop technique and rhythm before entering moving water or rapids. You should be able to move in a straight line without taking multiple strokes on one side at a time for correction. Course correction can be made by simply stroking a bit further from the side of the canoe using a modified or regular sweep stroke.

6. TURNING & CORRECTIVE MOVES

Sweep Strokes:

All of us who stand tall and carry a big stick need to have the ability to change direction quickly or to make angle corrections at some point in our travels. Proper technique and effective leverage accomplish these tasks with a minimum of strokes and energy. The pole can be used to gain leverage for hull alignment from the water or off the bottom, whether running down a wave train of standing waves, climbing upstream through complex rock gardens or just spinning to turn while in flatwater.

Sweeps are probably the most important strokes used in poling since draws and pries are not possible. They are very effective for eddy turns and peel-outs because they provide forward power as well as turning force.

The sweep stroke, whether paddle or pole, is one of the most poorly executed strokes by many boaters. What should be a 180-degree range of motion often turns into 140 degrees or less.

Boaters are often sloppy in starting the stroke about 20-30 degrees away from the bow and ending it just as far away from the stern. They don't take advantage of the powerful turning phase in the stroke but instead preserve only the forward portion of the stroke, which often sends the boater speeding ahead into trouble without any of the desired turning force.

Remember that the first and last 45 degrees of a full sweep provide the greatest amount of leverage for turning. The middle 90 degrees are mostly forward propulsion.

Here is a breakdown of the sweep stroke:

- Place your hands on the pole at shoulder width or a little wider if comfortable. Position is similar to holding a kayak paddle. The pole should be held waist high. Grip the pole as you would a kayak paddle, both thumbs on the inside, shoulder width apart.

- Extend (sliding the pole through your hands) the pole full length to one side so that the offside hand is gripping the end of the pole. If extending the pole to the right, the left hand grips the end. The onside hand is over the water while the offside hand is waist high in front of your midsection.
- Extend the far end of the pole in a near horizontal position with one to two feet inserted into the water as far ahead of the bow as possible.
- Sweep the pole around in a full arc of 180 degrees keeping the wet end as far away from the pivot point of the canoe as is possible. The further the pole's leverage end is from the canoe, the greater the turning torque. Both arms and hands will extend over the water (outside the canoe) as the pole completes its range of motion and reaches the stern, thus creating an increase of leverage.
- Torso rotation should occur during all sweeps to take advantage of the strong back muscles and their greater power for creating torque. The polers head and chest should follow the rotating pole such that a "box" is created between the pole, arms and chest that should be maintained throughout the range of motion. A wider range of pole motion also results from the upper body rotation.

Range of Motion in the Forward Sweep:

In analyzing the sweep angle, lets assume the bow is 0 degrees and the stern is 180 degrees. The bow also marks the 360-degree point at the end of the complete circle.

- **0 to 45 degrees**: (Fig 12a)The pole starts rotating away from the hull in a lateral (sideways) motion and pushes the bow in the opposite direction.

Turning and Corrective Moves

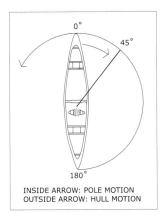

Fig 12a

INSIDE ARROW: POLE MOTION
OUTSIDE ARROW: HULL MOTION

Fig 12b

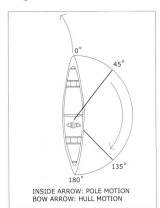

INSIDE ARROW: POLE MOTION
BOW ARROW: HULL MOTION

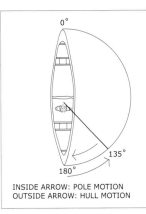

Fig 12c

INSIDE ARROW: POLE MOTION
OUTSIDE ARROW: HULL MOTION

Fig 12d

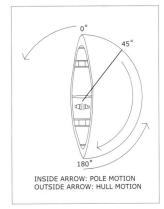

INSIDE ARROW: POLE MOTION
OUTSIDE ARROW: HULL MOTION

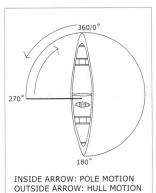

Fig 12e

INSIDE ARROW: POLE MOTION
OUTSIDE ARROW: HULL MOTION

Fig 12f

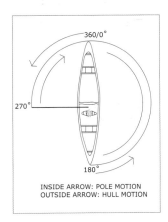

INSIDE ARROW: POLE MOTION
OUTSIDE ARROW: HULL MOTION

- 45 to 135 degrees: (Fig 12b) Rather than creating lateral leverage on the hull, this portion of the sweeping arc creates more forward motion on the canoe and is very helpful in maintaining momentum while changing direction. It also prevents the canoe from being pushed downstream by the current when turning upstream as it keeps the forward momentum heading upstream.
- 135 to 180 degrees: (Fig 12c) The pole sweeps toward the stern. This action pulls the stern laterally toward the pole and swings the stern under the bow. As the most powerful part of the sweep, this phase generates the greatest amount of torque and turning force on the canoe.
- 0 to 180 degrees: (Fig 12d) By incorporating the above listed portions you start by pushing the bow laterally away from the pole and pulling the stern sideways towards the pole completing the spin.
- 270 to 360/0 to 180 degrees: (Fig 12e)This powerful application is accomplished by reaching over the bow using a cross draw motion and pulling the bow towards the pole (the motion is the same as when conducting an offside eddy turn. Plate 15). The stroke draws the bow toward the pole. Upon reaching the bow, the poler quickly lifts the pole over the hull and reenters the water next to the canoe to complete the remaining 180-degree sweep.

On the cross draw, you can reach as far as 270 degrees for extra power, (Fig 12 f) but you need good flexibility and balance. The twisting action and ensuing leverage (Plate 14) can create some uncomfortable stress on the upper torso, knees and ankles. There's also the potential for a loss of balance and an unexpected swim if the excessive twisting force on the lower body causes your feet to slip.

Canoeists must generate just enough force to accomplish the desired move. Sweeping the last 45 degrees, from 135 to 180, is sometimes enough to make a quick angle correction. In other situations an application of 90 to 180 degrees is required for forward momentum as well as turning. For radical turns needing an immediate spin, a full 180 degrees or even 270 degrees is necessary.

Polers usually get into trouble after instituting a sloppy sweep with a range of motion of only 45 to 165 degrees when trying to turn. They become frustrated by the boat's reluctance to turn and fail to realize that they are not negotiating a full range of motion or incorporating the most powerful portion of the sweep stroke. (Plates 9/10/11) They end up using the middle portion of the sweep stroke, which is creating more forward speed than turning motion, and continue with additional incomplete sweeps. They end up driving the canoe straight into a rock or the bank because more forward power is being delivered than turning action on the hull.

In all cases un-weighting the offside of the boat when spinning enhances the turn. The lean creates rocker and reduces frontal resistance against the boat's leading edge as it spins. This reduces drag and keeps the leading edge of the canoe from being sucked under, causing an upset.

Reverse Sweeps

Reverse sweeps, 180 to 0 degrees, are very useful for negotiating a quick turn in the opposite direction. Hand motion and grip remain the same. The sweep starts from the stern and moves towards the bow.

I find it awkward to continue the sweep past 90 degrees because of weak and inefficient leverage from pushing forward on the pole rather than pulling. (Plates 12/13) I also don't recommend reverse sweeps when you're moving upriver against the current because it slows the canoe too much due to the reverse thrust being created on the hull, thus pushing it backwards downstream.

A larger range of motion is possible by over-rotating the body and beginning the reverse sweep from the 200-degree mark before sweeping the pole toward the bow. The length of the pole (and the extra height from standing up in the boat) will allow you to pass the pole over the stern and continue the sweep toward the bow without lifting the pole from the water.

To create a more explosive reverse sweep, you can lay the pole's grip end (approximately two to three feet from the end) on your onside hip, which is used as a fulcrum. Then push your hip out as you pull the pole in with your offside hand, which creates much greater leverage on the water. Grip the pole with one hand on each side of your hip to initiate the action.

A 360-degree motion can be accomplished with a combination of moves.

Let's try it on the left side of the canoe:

- Begin with a reverse sweep (180 to 270 degrees), and then quickly shift your hands into a cross-draw position when the pole is perpendicular to the canoe's midline.
- To do this you release your right hand from the pole while swinging your left hand with the pole up past your head and behind your body into the cross draw position (the wet end of the pole remains in the water throughout this move).
- Your right hand re-grips the pole just below the left hand with your palm facing downward.
- The left hand releases the pole and re-grips the end of the pole with the palm facing downward and with thumbs on the inside (kayak grip) facing each other.
- The cross draw sweep continues (270 to 360/0 degrees) to the bow, over the bow and then into a forward sweep on the other side (0 to 180 degrees).

This move creates a very powerful and fast spinning action on the canoe. It is also a very impressive move once you have it mastered.

Bottom Plant Turns:

In shallow water you can plant your pole on the bottom for leverage to produce powerful 180-degree turns and spins. This is much more effective than trying to use water based sweeps as there is no slippage of the pole when it is using water for leverage. The pole is set firmly on the bottom and then pulled in towards your body using your lower onside hand while pushing forward and away with your offside upper hand in a forward sweeping motion to create hull spin. As long as the pole does not slip off the bottom, the boat will spin quickly.

Lets go through the steps to make this happen correctly:

- Plant the pole four to six feet off the side of the canoe at about a 45 to 60 degree angle and well forward of the center thwart. The upper grip hand should be at eye level with the lower onside hand gripping roughly two feet lower. Note that the lower hand may move up or down on the pole depending on where the most effective leverage is gained at the moment of execution. Hand position should be using the kayak grip so thumbs are facing one another.
- Un-weight the opposite gunwale to create rocker and to eliminate frontal resistance against the leading edge of the canoe with a buildup of water on the offside as the canoe spins in that direction (the boat edge nearest the pole plant is weighted). Use the weighted foot to help push the bow around.
- Apply leverage to spin the canoe. The offside hand (on the high end) pushes against the pole while the lower hand pulls to create a turning force on the canoe, forcing the bow to lead the canoe in a tight turning motion. Use the offside rocker to change the shape of the wetted surface area on the hull to help the canoe to spin or turn quickly. Changing the hull shape can allow you to carve your turn much like a shaped ski.
- You should push the weighted knee and foot (nearest the pole plant) forward to help drive the bow around by transferring the force generated from the pole to the boat itself. This motion is similar to a skier who weights the right ski in a snowplow turn, and then turns to the left as a result.
- As the stern of the canoe reaches the pole, release the leverage and replant the pole forward of the center thwart to continue the turn.
- Another application is to use a planted cross draw for a

full 270-degree turn. In this case we will add an additional 90-degree extension to the 180-degree turn that was described above. This is a very powerful turn but you need good flexibility and balance. The twisting action on your body will try to force your feet to slip out of position, thus losing your balance and taking a swim. Here are the steps for adding the additional 90 degrees.

- Extend the pole out to one side so that you are holding the pole parallel to the surface of the water with the offside hand holding the end of the pole. Your hands should be on each side of your body, a little more than shoulder width apart.
- Twist your upper body so that the pole crosses over the bow and then another 90 degrees before planting the pole on the bottom in the cross draw position.
- The pole is near vertical. Pull the bow toward the pole by pulling in towards your body with the lower onside hand and pushing out on the pole with the upper offside hand. When the bow reaches the pole, release pressure on the pole and then lift the pole over the bow and replant it on the bottom. At this point, initiate the remaining 180-degree turn as described above. Don't forget to use upper torso rotation to create stronger force and a wider range of motion.

With these techniques and a little practice, you should be able to change direction quickly and effectively.

7. EDDY TURNS

A major accomplishment (and source of anxiety) for every beginning whitewater canoeist is avoiding rocks that suddenly appear out of nowhere. As skills and confidence develop, those same rocks become exciting challenges behind which you can execute eddy turns.

Eddy turns and peel outs (Plate 16) are not only fun but are also necessary skills for the accomplished boater. The ability to leave the main flow and seek protection behind an obstruction using an eddy turn is crucial. The ability to reenter the main current without capsizing while using a peel out is equally important. It affects proper negotiating of complex rock gardens, the ability to assist with rescue operations, avoiding potentially dangerous routes and the ability to take a breather when things are not going well.

Effective eddy moves have two components, an understanding of water dynamics and the physical ability to spin the canoe. A symbiotic relationship exists between the two components. One is unable to function effectively without the other.

Lets explore the dynamics of each and how to blend them together.

Eddy Currents:

An eddy is created by anything that obstructs the path of moving water such as boulders, ledges, and inconsistencies in the riverbank. (fig 13) Bends in a river cause eddies on the inside of the turn. As water hits an obstruction and is displaced by it, a void is created behind the obstacle. As the hollow attempts to fill itself, the water swirls into it from downstream and actually creates an upstream current behind the obstacle. The two opposing currents, the main downstream flow and the upstream

Canoe Poling

eddy current, create a current differential which is visible, called the eddy line which is where the two currents meet each other. A canoe that properly crosses this line spins due to the opposing forces acting on the hull, each one pushing the bow and stern in two opposite directions. It is important for the boater to understand and take advantage of the strongest part of the eddy just behind the obstruction which is caused by the lower elevation difference as water swirls in from behind in an attempt to fill in the depression. The upstream eddy current gets weaker and weaker the farther away from the obstruction you get as the immediate depression has been filled in and the river is now a consistent level.

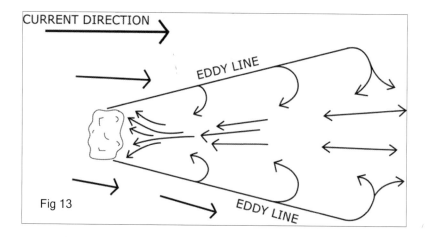

Fig 13

Eddy Turns:

Eddy turns are to canoeing what linked turns are to skiing. The boater's ability to control the river is similar to how a downhill skier controls steep terrain. Each person uses turns to control speed and for traversing desired routes of descent. There have been significant technical changes in how a poler negotiates an eddy turn as a consequence of competition requiring eddy turn techniques that are faster and more efficient. This has resulted in more continuous motion of the canoe and not allowing it to come to a complete stop at the top end of the eddy turn as was the previous case with the leverage eddy turn.

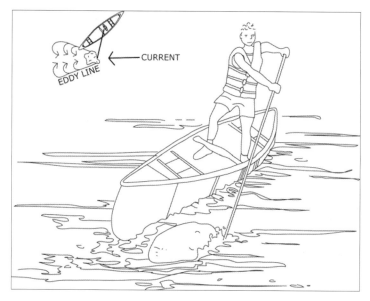

Fig 14

Let's first break down the components necessary for the canoe to enter the eddy:

- •The canoe should enter the eddy at an approximate 45-degree angle to the eddy line so that the current differential can exert turning force on the hull. (Fig 14)
- •The bow will be pushed upstream once it crosses the eddy line while the stern continues to swing downstream, until the entire canoe rests in the eddy water and is parallel to the upstream eddy current.
- • The bow should enter as close as possible to the top of the eddy to take advantage of the strongest force of the eddy and the current differential. This positioning initiates the spin by the eddy current holding the bow in place while the stern swings around due to being pushed downstream by the main current.

Canoe Poling

- Canoe speed has to be controlled when entering the eddy or the craft may overshoot it and leave the eddy before the spin begins. Momentum is important however because the main current can sweep the boat past the eddy if it lacks enough forward force to enter the eddy.
- The canoeist must also start the turning motion just before entering the eddy to allow the canoe to spin more easily as the current differential starts to work on the hull.

The size and power of the eddy determines the speed and angle of entry. The stronger the eddy, the sharper the angle and the higher the speed that can be used for successful entry. If an eddy is small or weak, the canoe must be almost perpendicular to the eddy line with limited forward speed to ensure entry. Be careful with particularly strong eddies as they can create an unstable base of water for the canoe to rest in because of currents swirling up from the river bottom.

Now let's explore the use of the pole in helping to execute the eddy turn:

There are actually two types of turns which can be utilized, the leverage eddy turn and the carving eddy turn. We will start with the leverage eddy turn.

- As the canoe approaches the top of the eddy with the proper angle of entry, you should quickly extend or swing the pole in front of you as if you were going to start a forward sweep to the downstream side of the boat.
- Grip the end of the pole with your offside hand and place the onside hand a little more than shoulder width apart towards the center of the pole, using the kayak grip.
- Just as the hull starts to cross the eddy line, you can

give a quick forward quarter sweep and then lift the pole over the bow in a cross draw motion and position it against the upstream side of the rock.
- Now apply leverage to help force the bow against the downstream side of the rock and hold it in place.

A word of caution is very important here:

As leverage is applied against the rock, quite a bit of twisting torque is placed on the person's body before the canoe starts to respond which may cause your feet to slip and cause you to fall or even wet exit the canoe.

As the end of the canoe starts to swing downstream, you should start weighting the offside (inside) leg (upstream side) to cause the boat to lean into the turn (like a bicycle leaning into a sharp corner). This un-weighting of the outside edge of the canoe prevents it from grabbing water, being sucked under and capsizing the boat. The lean also changes the hull configuration in the water by reducing the wetted surface area by lifting the ends, creating more rocker and allowing easier spinning.

Usually a forward sweep stroke should be used just before entering the eddy to help initiate the turn. With particularly powerful eddies, sweep strokes will drive the bow into the eddy while the main current swings the stern around downstream without requiring any leverage on the rock. Make sure you have angled the boat properly with enough lean.

The leverage eddy turn is a highly effective turn although its one downside is that all forward momentum and continuing turning is lost because of the pole holding the bow in place just behind the rock. While not a problem in general river running, it is not effective for competition due to the need to keep the bow leading the canoe through the turn with a continuous radius motion as you set up for the peel out and then exit the eddy.

Now lets discuss the technique required for the carving eddy turn:

Many of the concepts are the same as the leverage eddy turn, however pole position and leans are exactly the opposite of the leverage eddy turn.

- As the canoe approaches the top of the eddy with the proper angle of entry, you should quickly extend or swing the pole in front of you as if you were going to start a forward sweep. The pole should again be on the downstream side of the canoe.
- Grip the end of the pole with your offside hand while the onside hand should be gripping a little more than shoulder width apart towards the center of the pole, using the kayak grip.
- Now initiate a quick and powerful forward quarter sweep of only the first 45 degrees to start pushing the bow upstream but leaving the pole in position to quickly gain purchase on the river bottom.
- Just as the hull starts to cross the eddy line, push the end of the pole into the water and plant the pole on the river bottom on the inside of the eddy on the downstream side of the canoe.
- Just as you start to gain contact with the river bottom, you should switch your grip from a kayak grip to a batter's grip by reversing the offside hand so that both thumbs are facing up towards the sky to allow for proper leverage to take place.
- Once you make solid contact with the river bottom and the bow has crossed the eddy line, weight the onside foot to reduce the wetted surface area and to change the hull configuration in the water to create more rocker by pulling the two ends of the canoe out of the water. This will create a natural curvature of the hull so that the hull will start to carve and take advantage of both the eddy line differential force and the turning tendency that you have initiated.
- Lean heavily on the pole for balance and use your feet to help push the canoe through its turn. You will be pushing forward with the onside foot and pulling backwards with the offside foot.

- Apply leverage on the pole by pulling backwards with the lower onside hand and pushing forward with the top offside hand to help force the bow around.

If done correctly, the canoe will carve through its turn and naturally leave the eddy, reentering the main current to finish its peel out. This is a very fast, efficient and time saving maneuver.

Caution:

Be careful with how much you weight the onside (outside) edge of the canoe and the amount of speed you are carrying into the eddy as the edge of the chine will grab the water suddenly as the canoe starts to carve its turn, and throw you out of the canoe into the river. This can be very sudden as you are unnaturally leaning towards the outside of the turn rather than trying to counteract centrifugal force by leaning into and banking the turn as is the case with the leverage turn.

8. PEEL OUTS

Many of the same principles apply to peeling out of an eddy. Angles, leans and eddy line placement are the same.

We will first discuss the techniques for leaving the eddy after using the leverage eddy turn technique to enter the eddy.

- Establish a 30 - 45 degree angle of the canoe to the eddy line in preparation for exiting just behind the rock.
- Use one forward power plant (thumbs up with a batters grip) on the upstream side of the canoe to drive the boat halfway across the eddy line to take advantage of the current differential.
- Having the pole on the upstream side of the canoe is a change from earlier techniques that placed the pole on the downstream side of the canoe. You have to be able to break the suction of the eddy and keep from being sucked against the side of the rock due to the water swirling in to fill the eddy depression.
- Now quickly replant the pole downstream of the boat on the opposite side about four to six feet away from the canoe on the eddy line or just inside the eddy. You should be using the batter's grip with both thumbs on top facing the sky.
- The onside hand should be extended straight down the pole with a slight break in the elbow while the offside hand is placed at chin or eye level (holding the end of the pole), generally still a little more than shoulder width apart.
- Lean on the pole for balance and un-weight the offside gunwale (upstream side) to partially expose the boat's

bottom. The downstream main current will jet the bow around by pushing against the exposed bottom of the hull while the opposing eddy current pushes the stern upstream, thus spinning the canoe.

- Exit near the top of the eddy but far enough away from the rock so the stern has room to swing around without hitting it which is common, thus slowing or stopping the turn.
- The canoe will now enter the main flow while pivoting around the planted pole.
- The hull must spin into the main downstream current or the boat will stall on the eddy line or remain in the upstream eddy current.
- Complete the peel out by converting the function of the planted pole which is being used for balance to pivot around, into a forward power plant to accelerate out of the eddy and reach the speed of the current to help pick your line of travel.
- Make sure you are allowing the canoe to rotate around the pole to reenter the main current. A common mistake beginners make is to keep pushing against the pole while the canoe is broadside to the current, thus stopping its turn and completely stalling, half in and out of the eddy.
- Remember, the pole is only used for balance and to create a fulcrum point for the canoe to spin around. Don't apply leverage on it and end up trying to push the canoe sideways upstream against the current.

When peeling out of powerful eddies, cross draw strokes and/or sweep strokes are often enough to pivot the boat once the eddy line is crossed. Care must be taken to compensate for the downstream flow which, when in contact with the upstream side of the hull, will try to suck it under and cause a capsize by rolling the canoe upstream. Downstream boat lean is very important to avoid this.

Now lets discuss the technique required for the carving turn peel out:

This is where you will quickly see the speed advantage of this style over the leverage turn peel out due to its efficiency.

- As the canoe spins toward the top of the eddy after crossing the current differential, the pole should still be placed well within the eddy where you originally placed it in preparation for the start of the eddy turn.
- You should be gripping the end of the pole with the offside hand in a batter's grip with thumbs up and hands a little more than shoulder width apart.
- With the pole planted on the river bottom to the outside of the turning radius, you are able to keep the hull in motion and rotating in a circle.
- You will now leave the eddy and reenter the main current by applying leverage on the pole by pulling back with the lower onside hand and pushing forward with the top offside hand. The same leverage should be taking place with your feet as the weighted onside foot (outside edge) pushes forward and the un-weighted offside foot pulls back to help push the bow around.
- The weighting of the onside foot helps to reduce the wetted surface area and to change the hull configuration in the water to create more rocker by pulling the two ends of the canoe out of the water. This will create a natural curvature of the hull so that the hull will start to carve and take advantage of both the eddy line differential force and the turning tendency that you have initiated.
- Lean on the pole for balance and use your feet to help push the canoe through its turn.

If done correctly, (Fig 15) the canoe will carve through its turn and naturally leave the eddy, reentering the main current to finish the peel out. This is a very fast, efficient and time saving maneuver.

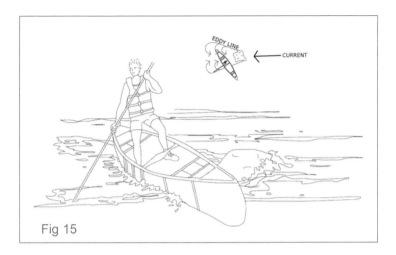

Fig 15

Caution:

Be careful with how much you weight the onside (outside) edge of the canoe and the amount of speed you are carrying into the main current, as the powerful downstream current will suddenly grab the edge of the upstream chine as the canoe starts to carve its turn, flipping the canoe and throwing you out of the canoe into the river. This can be very sudden because you are unnaturally leaning towards the turn rather than trying to counteract the centrifugal force by leaning into (or away) from the turn and banking the canoe, as is the case with the leverage turn.

When entering particularly heavy current, leaning to the outside is very dangerous for remaining upright. A modification to the outside leaning technique is to keep the pole planted on the outside of the turning radius to allow the hull to still rotate through its turn and cross the eddy line. As the hull reenters the strong current, quickly move the pole into a forward cross draw position with the pole placed on the downstream side of the canoe and drop the power end of the pole into the water. Let the water grab the power end of the pole and then with a little leverage, pull the bow towards the power end of the pole while gently leaning away from the turn to allow the water to slide under the hull until you are fully reentered into the main current and heading downstream again. At that time quickly reposition the pole into a forward power plant to accelerate to the speed of the current.

Using Leans to Turn:

It is fascinating to watch the technique of a new energetic racer against that of a seasoned and experienced racer. It is usually a contest of strength and power versus technique and finesse. The seasoned competitor uses years of experience to help shave seconds off his or her time. This translates into an understanding of moving water and how to make the canoe respond effectively. It has often been said by many racers who are well into their careers that they wish they knew then what they know now! Where these competitors once relied on power to perform moves, they now save time and energy with an educated approach. They read water conditions and use the shape of their canoe to react quickly. They are able to minimize mistakes and recover quickly from the ones they do make. An important part of their "education" is knowledge of the design shape of the hull and how it affects the boat's response. There are several factors which allow this to happen which we will explore.

9. DESIGN FACTORS

The influence of the canoe design has a major effect on both speed and maneuverability. The key aspects are rocker, chine and hull shape.

Rocker:
Is the amount of banana shape that is built into the bottom of the canoe. The more the ends turn up, the shorter the waterline and less frontal resistance that is created on the side of the canoe as it spins. Weighting one side of the canoe can create rocker. Because of the curved design of the side as it is tilted, the ends will naturally lift out of the water. This reduces the wetted surface area, which shortens the waterline and allows a quicker spin due to the side hull curvature.

Chine:
Is defined by Webster as "the juncture of the bottom and either of the sides of a boat". The amount of chine a canoe has

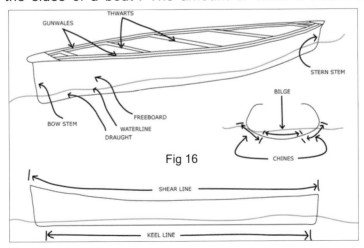

Fig 16

determines how effectively it can be used. The sharper the chine, the more it can be edged into the water to carve a turn. This is done by weighting the offside chine (right side if it is a left turn) so that it catches the oncoming water that forces the craft around. Canoes with bottoms that are flat, V-shaped, or modified V's are most effective because of their pronounced edge. Round bottoms have a diminutive edge so they are not able to slice into the water as well. Decked kayaks and canoes have long used this technique because of their pronounced edge.

Hull shape:

Is influenced by the width of the center thwart that pushes out the canoe sides and creates a natural rocker or curvature to the hull. As the canoe travels through water, it encounters equal frontal resistance on each side of the bow. If the canoe is tilted to one side, its shape in the water is like that of a protractor with a straight edge on one side and a curve on the other. Because the resistance is only on the side of the curvature, the hull naturally turns in the direction of the curve.

Marathon open canoe racers commonly use offside leans to minimize correction strokes and to change direction. The fuller the shape of the hull, the quicker the canoe responds. Marathon and Olympic canoes are very sleek with almost a straight line from the bow to the widest point and back to the stern. As a result they are less responsive than a recreational canoe with its greater flare beginning at the bow.

Manual Application:

Now lets take our knowledge of design factors and apply it to actual maneuvers. Our ultimate goal is to become one with our canoe to achieve efficiency and top performance. Let's look at how to integrate these moves.

Eddy turns:

There are two ways to enter an eddy to negotiate an eddy turn. The first is to angle in at about 45 degrees and then lean or bank the canoe into the turn as you would on a bicycle by weighting the inside edge of the boat. This counters the centrifugal force as the canoe carves its turn and spins into the eddy due to the twisting force on the hull from the current differential after crossing the eddy line. By banking the canoe, the stems or ends of the canoe lift out of the water, which reduces the wetted surface area and the canoe quickly spins around on the rounded side of the hull.

The second way is to angle in as described above at a 45 degree turn but after crossing the eddy line, weight the outside edge of the canoe so that the canoe is leaning to the outside of the turn as it begins its spin due to the current differential. You are again breaking the stem of the canoe out of the water which reduces resistance on the hull as it starts to spin. The natural curvature of the hull works in your favor for automatically carving a turn.

You have to be careful however with the speed that you enter the eddy as you can very easily flip the canoe due to the difficulty of controlling your centrifugal force that naturally wants to capsize the canoe. The outside edge of the canoe will naturally dig in and carve a turn due to its natural shape making for a very powerful, but somewhat risky technique.

Peel Outs:

Just as with eddy turns, there are two ways to exit an eddy. The first is to set an angle of about 45 degrees prior to accelerating out of the eddy into the main current and then lean or bank the canoe into the turn as you would on a bicycle by weighting the inside edge of the boat. This counters the centrifugal force as the canoe carves its turn and spins into the main flow due to the twisting force on the hull from the current differential after crossing the eddy line.

By banking the canoe, the stems or ends of the canoe lift out of the water, which reduces the wetted surface area and the canoe quickly spins around on the rounded side of the hull.

The second way is to angle out as described above at a 45 degree turn, but after crossing the eddy line, weight the outside edge of the canoe so that the canoe is leaning to the outside of the turn as it begins its spin due to the current differential.

You are again breaking the stems of the canoe out of the water which reduces resistance on the hull as it starts to spin. The natural curvature (protractor shape) of the hull works in your favor for automatically carving a turn.

You have to be careful however with the power and speed of the main flow as you can very easily flip the canoe due to the difficulty of controlling your centrifugal force and the force of the downstream current which will try to suck your upstream edge under and capsize the canoe. The outside edge of the canoe will naturally dig in and carve a turn due to its natural shape making for a very powerful, but somewhat risky technique.

This technique should really only be used in lower water conditions when the power of the current is significantly reduced and more easily controlled.

Upstream correction:

Bow control for polers pushing upriver in heavy water can be a significant challenge. If the bow drifts off center, the canoe may ferry to the side or get pushed downstream. To counter this effect, you must immediately plant the pole off to the downstream side of the canoe to hold it in place so it is not pushed backwards and to control any further loss of direction. Once your position is stabilized you should weight the downstream edge of the canoe while leaning on the pole. The canoe will immediately begin to point back upstream into the main current as the pressure from the water on the upstream side of the hull is released and the approaching water can slide off the bottom of the canoe. Applying leverage on the pole at the same time also helps push the bow back into position.

Straight line correction:

The canoe will tend to veer off course at times when you are attempting to propel it in a straight line.

Rather than take time to apply corrective action you can simply weight the opposite edge of the canoe to the desired direction of travel so that the protractor effect will then allow the canoe to carve around.

For example, weight the right side of the canoe if the canoe drifts to the right. This action releases any resistance on the left side so that the natural curvature and the frontal resistance on the right side of the hull will force the canoe to the left.

A fun exercise:

To help master this technique is to position the canoe heading upstream in some heavy flow.

- Plant the pole behind you and hold the canoe in one place against the current.
- Then slowly start to weight and un-weight each side of the canoe, feeling how the canoe will immediately veer to the opposite side of the lean as the resistance on that side of the hull is released.
- Use your feet to help push the hull in the direction you want the bow to move towards. You should be able to, without moving your pole, remain in one spot on the river and carve the hull back and forth simply by weighting and un-weighting each side of the canoe.

As with anything, this all takes time to master. However, once mastered, it will add a new dimension to your boating control and technical ability. You will find eddy moves and upstream travel much easier as you begin to let the design of the canoe work for you.

10. FERRYING

Lateral Moves:

Ferries are a critical skill for canoe polers to master whether their objective is racing or just plain fun. Crossing a river by ferrying is a common maneuver and an important part of a polers repertoire of skills.

Effective ferrying is necessary when scouting rapids, running a river or trying to shave seconds while racing. It lets you tap the river's energy and use it to supplement your own power. You will experience an enormous sense of control and accomplishment by moving across strong current without losing position on the river or getting blown downriver by the current. Let's define the two basic ferries.

Forward ferry:

You are facing upstream in the standard position with the bow as the upstream end of the craft. Forward power plants will counter the downstream force of the current to allow you to hold your position on the river, relative to the shoreline.

You must weight the downstream side of the canoe as was described in the previous chapter to allow the water to slide off the upstream side of the canoe. By exposing the upstream side of the canoe and pointing the bow in the direction you want to move, the approaching water will push it towards the side of the river you wish to move towards. The lighter upstream end will offer less resistance and make the ferry easier to control.

Back ferry:

The canoe is moving slowly (slower than the main current) downstream with the poler facing downstream in the standard position with the stern as the upstream end of the craft. The canoe should be angled so that the upstream end is pointed towards the shore you are trying to ferry to. The current will contact the exposed upstream side and push it sideways. By weighting the downstream side of the canoe, it will move faster in the desired path of travel, as more of the upstream side of the hull will be exposed for the current to push against.

If you are standing behind the center thwart, then the upstream end of the canoe will be weighted and it will be hard to control and want to swing downstream.

Using the pole as a rudder in front of you and positioned on the downstream side of the canoe will be crucial for controlling the upstream end of the canoe by pulling the downstream end of the canoe under the upstream end. If you are struggling to hold the upstream end of the canoe in place, then change the trim by stepping (or jumping) over the center thwart to weight the downstream end of the canoe which will lighten the upstream end, making it easier to control. Be careful when you are crossing the thwart as you can easily have an upset and end up swimming.

Snubbing and reverse kayak strokes will slow the boat's descent downstream.

If executed properly, ferries are simply a use of boat angles and current direction to provide lateral motion. The boat will move perpendicular to the current or diagonally downstream depending upon the river's speed and power in proportion to the amount of forward force you apply on the hull.

Three variables affect the success of ferries: boat angle, amount of generated power against the current, and pole plants. Let's assume in the following discussion that you are facing upstream and current direction is 0 degrees.

Canoe Angle:

Establishing proper boat angle is the less experienced polers biggest challenge. Lateral movement is created by exposing one side of the canoe to the current. Current strikes the upstream side creating lateral resistance and pushes the canoe towards the shore that the upstream end of the canoe is facing. (Fig 17)

Canoe Poling

Too little boat angle (0 to 5 degrees) will fail to expose enough of the side of the canoe to the current and it will stall.

Too much angle (70 degrees or greater) exposes too much of the side of the canoe and it will be pushed downstream broadside, out of control.

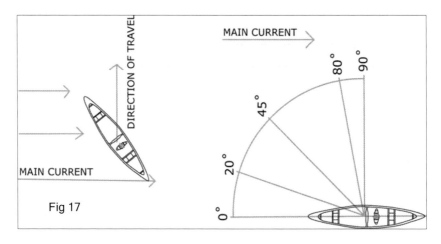

Fig 17

Keep the following factors in mind:

- Point the canoe's upstream end toward the chosen destination across the river.
- Know the direction of the main flow in determining proper boat angle.
- Be aware that current direction often changes due to eddies and physical topography of the river bottom as you cross the river and you may have to adjust your angle.
- Proper boat angle is between 20 and 70 degrees depending on the speed and power of the current.
- The stronger the current, the less angle necessary for the lateral push.
- Tighter angles (20-30 degrees) are easier to control and can be opened up if necessary. Wide angles are very difficult to close or reduce in heavy water and may

subject you to being pushed downstream sideways, a very dangerous and possibly costly move to your canoe.

- The wider the angle (30 to 70 degrees), the greater the hull exposure and the stronger the current's lateral push. Wider angles result in faster lateral movement.
- Capsizes often occur when leaving the eddy because the canoe is subjected to an opposing current trying to suck the upstream edge under, thus rolling the canoe over upstream.
- Use proper boat lean to minimize upsets (always lean downstream).

Leaving eddies deserves some caution. A good strategy is to begin with a small angle to get a feel for the current and then widen the angle if necessary. Leave the eddy quickly with good power and get the entire canoe into the main flow. If the boat straddles the eddy line too long, the main current can grab the upstream end and spin the boat around sending you downstream and possible causing a capsize.

Boat lean is crucial:

It should change as the canoe moves from the main current into the eddy because of the different directions of the two currents. The boat's upstream edge must be un-weighted at all times to prevent the current from sucking it under and upsetting the canoe.

Pole Plants:

You will usually find that the safest and most effective way to plant your pole once the ferry is underway is on the upstream side of the canoe (the side opposite the direction of travel).

This strategy prevents the canoe from moving into a planted pole upsetting the boat or bending the pole after you run over it. If you have to plant your pole on the downstream side to control downstream drift, extend the pole to its full length and plant it as far as possible from the canoe and keep in mind that the current will try to push the canoe into the pole.

Remember these basic principles:

- Plant the pole close to the canoe and two to three feet behind yourself on the upstream side of the canoe.
- Apply power in a diagonal direction to push the canoe both laterally and forward. The canoe should be moving away from the pole.
- Expend limited energy during the power phase. Power plants should only generate enough power to counter the downstream force of the main current and to push the canoe across the channel smoothly.
- Improper boat angle will send the canoe off course. The bow will usually try to swing downstream and you are then faced with a difficult correction back to the proper angle.
- Extend your pole on the downstream side and use 180-degree sweeps for correction. The combination of forward power and corrective action will drive the bow upstream while pulling the stern back under the bow.
- Concentrate on the last 90 degrees of the sweep where you will be most effective in changing the boat angle. The canoe's upstream end usually has the strongest resistance against it because the main current strikes it first, causing considerable frontal resistance. It resists efforts to be pushed upstream. The downstream end encounters much less resistance because it is moving with the main flow and can be pulled much easier below the bow.

Forward Power:

Forward power is an integral part of effective ferrying. You will find that you have to change the amount of power required to follow your chosen route. The degree of power you use determines whether the boat moves perpendicular to the current or diagonally upstream or downstream.

Plate 14
The Cross draw requires the poler to twist their upper body
and reach over the bow to the opposite side of the canoe and
pull towards the pole. This is an effective and stable means of
turning the canoe into a heavy current when leaving and
eddy.

Plate 15
In the offside eddy turn the poler plants the pole on the downstream side with the pole placed inside the eddy line. Then
weights the onside (downstream side) allowing the edge of
the canoe to carve into the turn.

Plate 16
On a peel out the poler angles the canoe across the eddy line, the sets the pole downstream of the canoe on the eddy line, weights the onside to create rocker and allows the boat to spin using the current differential

Plate 17
Sideslipping requires the poler to weight the onside of the canoe while pushing away from the pole so that the approaching water slides off the bottom. The hands are in a batters grip with the pole placed perpendicular to the side of the canoe.

Plate 18
The poler leaves the eddy at a slight angle and powers the bow into the drop to get it to pop up on top of the drop.

Plate 19
The poler quickly resets the pole and drives the canoe up and over the drop.

Plate 20
The poler is now on top of the drop and quickly retrieves their pole to set up for the next power plant upstream.

Plate 21
Climbing drops is what separates polers from paddlers and requires both skill and technique

Plate 22
When climbing against a heavy current the poler should keep the pole between the shore and the canoe in order to push the stern out and the bow tucked in.

Plate 23
Snubbing downstream requires the poler to reposition their body in front of the centre thwart to create a bow heavy trim, with the pole extended in front of the polers body using a jabbing motion to control the downstream descent.

Remember these basis principles:

- Forward power and canoe speed must be equal to current speed to move perpendicular to the current.
- To move upstream, forward power and canoe speed must be greater than the current speed.
- To move downstream, forward power and canoe speed must be less than the current speed.

River Reading Skills:

As your physical skills improve, you will need to develop highly refined river reading skills for effective course navigation. These skills must be more exact than those of the average downstream paddler due to the difficulties of upstream movement. Upstream travel is dependent upon using the river power to one's advantage.

The river looks very different when viewed upstream as opposed to downstream. You have to recognize the backside of eddies for finding the weak trailing end of the eddy current, where eddy lines are, as well as looking for downstream V's from the closed end. You must be able to pick a line to run upstream using every eddy possible to gain some protection from the main flow. Try to take advantage of every situation possible to make it work to your benefit for moving upstream efficiently with a minimum expenditure of energy.

Here are several rules to keep in mind:

- Water generally runs slower and shallower near the shore than in the middle of a river channel on straight sections of river. This is due to friction between the water and the river bottom. Stay along the shore when poling upriver for protection against the main flow.
- Water naturally flows in as straight a line as possible. The only reason it changes direction is because the riverbed dictates where it goes based on the physical topography of the river bottom. Water will move to the

outside of a bend because it is trying to go straight and is forced to turn when it encounters the bank. The majority of the water is going to be on the outside of the bend making it the deepest part of the river channel and the fastest, most powerful water. For protection against the main flow and ease of travel, stay to the inside of a river bend to find shallow water and to catch upstream eddy currents when available. Eddies always exist on the inside of a river bend because the river is trying to fill in a void created from the main flow bypassing it as it runs to the outside of the bend.

- Because water moves in a straight line unless pushed in another direction, erosion always occurs on the outside of a bend. Beware of roots, downed trees causing strainers and trapped debris. Also be alert to the fact that the water is going to try to push and pin you against the outside shore where the greatest force of water is.
- When moving upstream, line up behind rocks in heavy water (no matter how far away) to gain protection from the main current. Trailing eddy water can extend quite a way downstream depending on the size and strength of the eddy, so use it to your advantage and try to get a little upstream help from the eddy current.
- Try to pick a route that allows leapfrogging and eddy hopping from rock to rock for constant protection from the current. This may involve ferries to make the move from rock to rock but it will also conserve energy when moving upstream.
- In shallow water conditions, use the opposite reasoning for picking a line to travel. Because the conditions are going to be scratchy, you will need every extra inch of water possible which will make the difference between floating or scraping through. Run to the outside of the bend where the deepest water is. Because of the low conditions and lack of water, there will be less force to push you against the outside bank.
- Recognize that water is going to follow the fall line

which is the path that a ball would take if you were to let it roll down a decline. As a result, water won't always move to the outside of a bend if there isn't enough power to force it there. It may move to the inside if the fall line draws it there because of how the river bottom is sculpted.

- When running downstream, take the exact opposite course as you would for poling upstream. You now want to take advantage of every amount of downstream power possible for maximum speed and to conserve energy. Avoid crossing eddy lines that will slow you down because of the upstream current and stay to the outside of the bend for the fastest, deepest water.

11. SIDE SLIPPING

Side slipping is an important skill for negotiating river position whether you are traveling upstream, downstream, or preparing to exit an eddy. You need to have the ability to move your double ended craft sideways to improve your angle and position for negotiating a particular section of river without losing either the canoe's parallel alignment to the current or being pushed backwards when moving upstream.

In paddling, you learn to use combinations of draws and pries to slide the canoe sideways. Because draws are impossible with a pole, you have to use the closest thing to a pry which is a lateral power plant. This skill comes in very handy when preparing to exit an eddy. You may have to move the canoe

Fig 18

sideways across the eddy to set up the peel out without changing the necessary angle for crossing the eddy line.

Side slipping (Fig 18) is a bit different depending on which direction you are heading in current so lets explore the factors involved with both.

Upstream:

When climbing upstream, you always have the current trying to push you back downstream. Side slipping is typically used to adjust your position prior to climbing a drop or for sliding into an eddy's wash to gain some protection from the main flow. When facing upstream, you have to contend with trying to move laterally as well as maintaining your present position.

The key is to plant the pole downstream of you to counteract the force of the current. The pole should be planted in close to the canoe to prepare for the power application and on the side of the canoe opposite the direction you wish to move towards. Hand position will be two to three feet apart with the offside (top) hand gripping the top end of the pole and being positioned just below your jaw next to the onside shoulder. The pole should have a 15 to 20 degree forward angle across the canoe in front of your body to allow for proper leverage to take place. As you start to apply power, un-weight the offside of the canoe to drop the onside gunwale close to the water. This action reduces the wetted surface area, breaks the bow stem out of the water shortening the water line, and allows water to slide off the bottom as the canoe moves sideways away from the pole. It also prevents the leading edge of the canoe from grabbing and rolling underwater (from increased frontal resistance on the side of the canoe as it moves laterally).

Use short power plants to move the canoe laterally. The plants should be in a diagonal direction to provide force both in the direction of travel and forward power to counteract the downstream push on the canoe. Use leg drive and pressure with your feet to help maintain the canoe's parallel position to the current. Make sure the pole exits the water cleanly after each plant to minimize any drag on the water. A modified pool cue recovery is best for repositioning the pole for the next plant.

Canoe Poling

Downstream:

Downstream movement requires quick reflexes and the ability to move the canoe sideways as you travel because the faster you move, the faster those pesky rocks seem to jump out in front of you. Side slipping is a bit different now because you are continuing to move forward with the current. It is more difficult to execute because the canoe is moving past the point of pole purchase with the bottom.

You have to plant the pole forward of the canoe so that it will provide some braking as well as lateral push as the canoe moves past it. There isn't as much lateral action on the hull as when the canoe is stationary because the forward motion is absorbing some of the lateral motion.

The un-weighting action probably won't be as accentuated because of the forward direction requiring more balance and stability than when moving the canoe from a stationary position. There should not be drastic side movement, as it usually requires only inches of movement to clear a rock.

It is important to keep forward speed under control to help negotiate complex routes. The faster you move, the faster things start to happen and the less time you have to compensate with correction.

Stationary water:

Calm water is the easiest to sideslip in, be it flat stretches of river or behind eddies. It is simply a matter of planting the pole next to the canoe so that it is perpendicular to the center line of the canoe and parallel to the center thwart. Weight the onside gunwale and push away from the pole keeping it at right angles to the midline of the canoe. Hand grip and position on the pole should be the same as described above.

Small power plants with pool cue recovery should be applied. An exaggerated, un-weighting motion is possible to help reduce the wetted surface area and surface friction, thus increasing the lateral movement after each power plant. Subtle pressure on the pole either forward or backward while applying power will help correct the canoe's angle if it starts to drift at all.

It is very important to master stationary water side slipping before applying it in moving water, so practice, practice, practice. (Plate 17) Find a good section of bottom on a pond or lake and line yourself up perpendicular to the shoreline and just practice moving sideways back and forth to gain control of your bow and the ability to keep the canoe totally perpendicular to the shoreline.

12. UPSTREAM TRAVEL

Upstream travel against heavy current and rapids is what separates canoe polers from paddlers and what provides that special feeling of accomplishment and victory against the ever-relentless downstream current. There is a tremendous sense of satisfaction in knowing that you are truly among a select few who can move effectively, efficiently and rapidly upstream.

There are a few talented paddlers who can make their way up some surprisingly difficult water but they are nowhere as fast or efficient. Most paddlers end up either lining up, wading in waist deep water, pushing and/or pulling their boat, or portaging up to quieter water upstream.

The upstream ability of poling creates true independence for boaters by eliminating the need for shuttles and providing a sense of self-sufficiency. For me it is the primary attraction of the discipline. Essentially we take the best the river has to offer and beat it at its own game by using that raw power to our advantage to help us move in harmony with the river.

The sense of satisfaction that rock climbers feel after conquering a difficult rock face is the way canoe polers feel after beating upstream against the relentless downstream flow of waves, heavy current, and a constant effort of the river to push the canoe backwards. I derive a natural euphoria from this very physical experience where I mentally, physically and emotionally meet the river on its own terms, defy normal standards of travel direction and reach the top of a rapid. This is all accomplished through a simple understanding of angles, leverage, river reading, and a willingness to be patient and work hard. Let's review how these different elements all play a part in effective upstream movement.

Bow Control:

The most essential component to successfully poling upstream is total control of your bow. It is a combination of the factors we just read about. Bow control is clearly the factor that separates top racers from the rest of the pack and what creates more frustration among canoeists trying to move upstream than anything else. There are three key elements to consider for proper bow control.

Trim:

Establishing proper canoe trim is the most important factor in successful bow control. You need to have a stern heavy trim so the bow stem breaks out of the water and does not track. Driving the bow into current creates very difficult control problems because as soon as you are just a few degrees off center, the canoe will begin to veer off course and head for shore at a rapid pace. The angle will usually increase once you lose it making it more difficult for correction.

You should be standing approximately one to two feet behind the center thwart based on the shape of the hull and your physical weight. Be aware of the tendency to creep forward and lean against the center thwart as it will only add weight to the bow and drive it into the current making it very hard to control. As the water difficulty increases, it may be necessary to move further back in the canoe to pick the bow up higher to clear the rough conditions.

Current alignment:

You must always have a sense of where the water is coming from, regardless of the riverbank configuration.

The canoe midline should always be parallel to the current direction so that equal force is striking both sides of the bow equally. Should the force become disproportionate in any way, the canoe will immediately veer off course at a speed proportionate to the current's power.

Constant observation of bubbles, leaves, sticks, eddy lines and river gradient is essential for proper assessment of water direction.

You will find that the current always has small changes as you move along which will require minimal amounts of correction because of eddy wash, river bed inconsistencies, channel movement and obstacles such as downed trees, boulders, flood debris and pinned canoes.

Pole plant alternatives:

Your bow control can be improved by hugging the shore and using a hand over hand power plant technique while executing all your pole plants between the canoe and the shore. This strategy will keep the bow tucked into the shore to prevent the current from pulling it back into the main flow because of your ability to push the stern out away from the shore if necessary.

If the bow starts to drift out, simply use the pole to push the stern out which will force the bow back in. The most effective means of power is by using short but powerful power plants to provide constant forward motion so that forward speed does not stall, otherwise the bow will start to slide out into the current.

The hand over hand technique with pool cue recoveries help produce constant forward power with less effort than using power plants, especially when climbing steep pitches.

In particularly difficult water, use short power plants on the shore side of the canoe with rapid and forceful pool cue recoveries that don't break the surface of the water (to reduce recovery time between plants) to keep the canoe from being pushed backwards.

As you become more adventuresome and powerful, moving right up the middle of the heavy current will be an inviting challenge. The cross over windmill recovery is necessary to maintain the constant bow correction demanded by stiff current. By alternating sides, you ensure forward movement and bow control. Power is generated and course direction is automatically corrected by generating force on each side of the canoe. This is a physically demanding approach.

Pole plants must always be placed behind you to gain leverage off the river bottom. If you allow the canoe to drift back after planting the pole, the pole will end up in a vertical position in front of you. As a result, you lose all your leverage and the boat will continue to drift downstream. A sudden lack of balance because of overextending yourself in a forward position will easily cause an unpremeditated wet exit from the canoe!

Exiting Eddies Upstream:

Part of effective upriver work is the use of eddy hopping. This practice of seeking protection from the main flow by using the upstream eddy current behind a boulder is an important component of making the river work to your benefit.

The only drawback is that it does position you behind boulders that may be very difficult to break away from if there is a powerful suction that will keep the canoe in the eddy and pinned against the rock. You must ensure a swift reentry into the main current so that the current differential has little opportunity to force the canoe drastically off course by spinning it because of the opposing forces being exerted on each end of the canoe.

The best strategy is using power plants on the eddy side of the canoe so that the pole plant is between the canoe and the rock as it is passed. This move ensures a breakaway from the rock and its eddy suction as well as providing strong forward movement of the canoe upstream.

Pole plants on the river side of the exiting canoe will only serve to pin the canoe against the rock, thus stopping forward progress and leaving the boat in unstable eddy wash, thus putting it in danger of taking on water if it is breaking over the top of the rock.

Climbing Drops:

As you move upriver, you will eventually come up against the same drops that paddlers love to run down through. Poling up over a drop is what makes the sport so challenging and exciting. It is the most exhilarating move you can make on the river. Many polers are intimidated by drops but they are not difficult if negotiated properly.

You first need to line up in the eddy at the bottom of the drop about two feet behind the ledge. Your canoe should be on the inside edge of the eddy line with just enough angle to break out of the eddy so that the canoe will be parallel with the main current as it leaves the eddy.

Once your re-entry angle is ready, use a very aggressive power plant to drive the bow out of the eddy and into the middle of the tongue of the chute. If there is enough forward momentum the bow will pop up on top of the tongue. A second rapid power plant or hand over hand plant will send the rest of the canoe up and over the drop to the next higher level. (Fig 19)

It is critical that the canoe's forward speed does not stall or you will be pushed down backwards.

Most drops are lined with boulders on each side of the tongue so use these to your benefit. It is perfectly acceptable to brace one side of your bow against one to help guide the canoe forward as you move up the chute.

Because the current picks up a great deal of velocity as it drops over the ledge, bow control can become much more difficult. As you improve your control, you should be able to climb drops without the aid of side boulders and move right up the middle of the chute.

Pinned poles are very common when climbing drops because of the amount of forward leverage you are placing on it. Poles have a tendency to jam between whatever cracks or crevices they come in contact with. As a result, you will come to a sudden stop that will make you feel like your arm is being torn out of its socket. If you have enough forward force, a pinned pole will yank you right out of your canoe. Nevertheless, your forward momentum will stop, making it very difficult to continue forward without driven back again. It is possible to push up from a dead stop while halfway into the tongue, but it requires a very strong power plant to overcome the current.

Drops up to three feet in elevation can be climbed easily. (Plates 18 to 22) Taller drops are difficult because water starts to pour into the boat as you bury the bow into the drop in an effort to get it to pop up on top. Because you are at right angles to the drop, you will torpedo the bow right into a tall drop with no chance of getting it to pop up. The boat loses all of its momentum and actually bounces back, causing you to lose your balance, thus falling forward or even out of the canoe.

Standing further back in the canoe will bring the bow up

Fig 19

higher to help break through but you may have to look for another drop that is cut with a flatter angle so that the bow will have a chance to enter and pop up and over.

The shape of the hull will also have a major impact on how well it climbs drops, as a fuller bow will tend to ride up and over much better than a narrow, sharp bow which will torpedo in without riding up as quickly, thus taking in more water.

13. DOWNSTREAM TRAVEL

Snubbing and Wildwater:

As you start downstream after a long, hard climb, it is reminiscent of the reward that a rock climber experiences when rappelling down after a tough climb or the sensation the cross country skier feels while skiing down a steep trail after a lengthy climb.

The biggest problem you will encounter will be controlling your speed for proper river reading and controlled navigation. The faster you move, the quicker things will start to happen, the faster rocks suddenly appear in front of you and the less time you have to correctly react to it. Here are two techniques you can use for effective downriver travel, one to control your speed and the other to maximize your speed using the current.

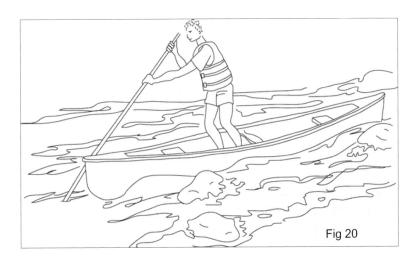

Fig 20

Snubbing:

This classic downstream technique uses short poling jabs called snubs where the pole is placed in front of you and essentially takes jabs at the bottom to control your speed and course direction. (Fig 20 & Plate 23)

Snubbing is typically used when descending technical rock gardens where there is very fast current and course correction is essential. Because of the many required changes in course direction, the poler is forced to negotiate a specific route while keeping the hull speed slower than the current.

Here are some helpful tips for effective snubbing.

- First change the trim of your canoe by standing in front of the center thwart and facing the bow (you should be looking downstream). Your distance from the center thwart is the same as if the boat were heading upstream, about one to two feet. By creating a bow heavy trim, the water will slide under the stern (upstream end) and keep the stem from tracking as the canoe slowly moves downstream.
- You should be in the power poling stance for maximum stability. You can also control the boat angle by using leg drive and pushing forward with one leg and then the other to help swing the upstream end sideways to maintain hull alignment. Maintaining a parallel relationship to the current is critical for boat control.
- Extend your pole directly in front of you with the pole along the onside of the canoe to prepare for the first snub.
- Your onside hand should be holding the top end of the pole and it should be at eye level.
- The offside hand is placed two feet lower down on the pole depending on comfort and effective leverage.
- Both hands should be in the batter's grip with thumbs on top.

Canoe Poling

- The pole angle is the same as when poling upstream, about 45 degrees depending upon the amount of forward speed and braking required. A flatter angle creates greater leverage off the bottom and increased braking power. The pole should be directly downstream of the canoe with a parallel alignment to the midline of the craft.
- As you move downstream, use short forceful snubs (or jabs) to control and slow your descent.

Be aware of the pole's tendency to jam between rocks because of the added pressure from the force of the canoe moving with the current.

As the canoe approaches the planted end of the pole, the pole angle will naturally increase as it moves more and more towards a vertical angle because of you moving closer to it. This will usually cause it to pin or jam between rocks because its exit angle is different from its entry angle. To counteract this you must use very quick and short snubs so that the pole is exiting at close to the same angle as it entered. When executed properly, you can achieve surprisingly tight control down very technical sections with no clear channels.

Wildwater:

This downriver technique is used to run courses at speeds equal to or greater than the river current. It works best in channels requiring limited course direction.

You stand directly behind the center thwart (facing downstream) to create a more streamlined waterline and trim as a result of dropping the bow down. Then you use forward power plants or kayak strokes to accelerate your forward velocity such that it is equal to or greater than the downriver current speed. Note that your pole will have a strong tendency to pin on the bottom when using power plants because of the radically changing exit angle due to the higher speed downstream.

Little problem exists with the weighted upstream end tracking because the canoe is moving faster than the current. In picking a course, you follow the main flow and avoid crossing any eddy lines because the upstream eddy currents will slow your forward progress downstream.

Quick changes in course direction are necessary when rocks suddenly appear. The most effective technique is side slipping to one side or the other as described earlier in this chapter. Remember to un-weight the offside to break any downward suction of the leading edge as the canoe moves laterally sideways towards the offside of the canoe. Then use short and forceful power plants perpendicular to the canoe to push or slide it sideways. These power plants may have to occur quickly at times with many changes of direction from side to side depending on how fast the rocks suddenly pop up in front of you.

When running through a river bend, take into consideration the lateral drift that occurs because of the water running straight against the shore on the outside of the bend. The water will try to push your canoe against the outside bend. You need to compensate for it by entering the bend on the inside third of the channel just outside the eddy line. As you move through the bend, you will drift closer and closer to the outside shore so if your alignment is right, you will exit the bend on the outside third of the channel in the fastest water but not so close as to worry about being pinned against the outermost bank.

Leg action is very important in downriver running because you are usually encountering waves, holes and pillows (rocks just under the surface not always noticeable until you are right on top of them). You need to have the balance and ability to weight and un-weight as you hit these disturbances to keep from taking in water and to allow the bow to pass over rocks just under the surface.

By un-weighting as you come up against a braking wave or haystack, you increase the height of the wave side of the canoe so that it is a higher obstacle for the wave to break over, thus taking in little if any water. When suddenly encountering rocks without having time to move laterally, simply un-weight the side of the canoe to create a reduced wetted surface area and narrowed water line width. The canoe will now pass right over the rock without impact or without creating any drag. This technique also allows you to pass through channels that are smaller than your normal water line width by allowing the canoe

Canoe Poling

to pass through on its side rather than with a full bottom profile.

With wildwater you should be prepared for the quick buildup of downriver speed. You have little time to analyze the river conditions and react to them properly. The most effective means of reducing speed and regaining control if necessary is to back paddle using a reverse kayak stroke. Remember, the slower you travel, the more control you will have.

14. REVERSE MOVES

An important skill to have whether poling or paddling is the ability to run down channels in reverse or to perform maneuvers backwards.

There are times when you may get spun around after hitting a rock or you don't complete a ferry and you have to run down backwards because there isn't time or room to pivot around.

The highest percentage of unexpected spills is when the canoe is perpendicular to the main current. Instead of only requiring channels the width of the canoe, you now need channels the length of the canoe, which are much tougher to find. Many boaters are nervous when they get turned around and feel that they should be facing forward to run a section of river.

The canoe doesn't care which end is leading as it moves downstream so just look over your shoulder as you move in reverse. With poling we are able to take it one step further, which is the ability to push upstream in reverse and believe it or not, it is a very useful and practical skill. Let's explore some of your options.

Running Downstream in Reverse:

There are many times when you will run a section downstream in reverse. In some cases it may be easier than running it in a forward position because you have tremendous braking capacity for controlling speed.

Keep yourself positioned as you would for upstream climbing and just look over your shoulder as you move downstream in reverse. The pole should be positioned behind you in the same position as snubbing except you are facing upstream rather than downstream. The principle is the same in that you use short, quick snubs to control your descent. You have to be conscious

89

of maintaining the same entry and exit angles of the pole to prevent it from pinning. If you feel you are descending too quickly, simply plant the pole and stop your progress. You can hold yourself stationary in moving water indefinitely as long as the canoe remains parallel to the main current. If you need to take a rest, ferry or side slip into the nearest eddy.

Make sure you have a stern heavy trim so the current will flow under the upstream end to prevent tracking. Watch for rocks just under the surface because, if hit, they can cause an immediate loss of balance, with you doing a seat plant on the bottom of the canoe or exiting out of the canoe prematurely.

Running Upstream in Reverse:

There are many times when you may be picking your way down a complex rapid only to hit a dead end. Usually there is no room to eddy out or turn so you are forced to back out.

If the current isn't too strong, you can remain in your power poling stance and simply start backing up. Position the pole in front of you as if you were going to snub and instead apply reverse power plants to start climbing upstream backwards.

You can use the pole as a rudder by leaving it in the water for a very short period of time after completing the power plant in front of you and move it left or right to correct your course.

The difficulty with this maneuver is that because you have not changed your trim, the stern or upstream end wants to track because it is weighted. You can control it, but it is tough and requires constant attention to keep the bow positioned under the stern.

An easier move to change your body position in the canoe so that you are on the opposite side of the thwart is to do a "Rock Hop" over the center thwart, (Fig 21) thus changing your trim immediately so the bow (downstream end) is now weighted. This is merely jumping over the center thwart so that you land in the same power plant position as previously except that you are facing the new stern. As you land, your feet should be against the chine of the canoe for stability and balance. You should still be one to two feet behind the thwart for proper trim. The original (upstream) stern is no longer tracking and will swing around at will. Your body positioning is exactly like the normal power poling stance except you are facing backwards.

Fig 21

Use the same principles for upstream climbs by crossing the pole over from side to side to generate power while maintaining bow (or in this case, stern control). Because you are close to the end of the canoe you have the ability to direct force on each plant by moving the top end of the pole left or right as you initiate the reverse power plant. The pole will pass over the end of the canoe if you raise up on the pole enough to cross it over the stem. It is amazing how effective you are in this position and you can run up surprisingly difficult water and even climb drops like this. Don't forget to look over your shoulder to see where you are going.

Another alternative, although you want to practice this in flatwater first, is to perform a "rock-a-copter" to change ends and direction in the canoe at the same time. (Fig 22) Once you realize that you have to back out, do a "Rock Hop" over the center thwart and while you are in the air, spin your body 180 degrees so that when you land, you will be perfectly positioned in the normal power poling stance and you can start climbing with the proper trim and body positioning.

Use caution when first trying this but once you have it, you will find it the quickest and most efficient means of repositioning yourself on the opposite side of the thwart in the canoe. And it

Canoe Poling

is a real crowd pleaser!

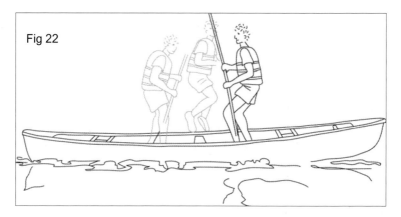

Fig 22

But practice first as it can have devastating consequences if your miss your jump and fall out of the canoe.

15. RACING

If you truly want to get better at whatever sport you pursue, get involved in competition and challenge yourself to race.

Racing should not be looked at as threatening or just something that only the elite level athletes are involved in. Racing forces you to apply the technique and form you have learned in this book and refine it in a fashion that allows you to be efficient while climbing tougher rapids and drops than you would expect.

There is nothing written here that isn't used or hasn't been finely tuned through competition. By attending races you are exposed to some of the best canoe polers in the country and a great deal of information and technique can be gleaned from them.

Take advantage of the existing opportunities to shorten your learning curve by being exposed to the top athletes in poling and seeing what is truly possible with a pole even though it may be beyond your existing abilities.

Learn first-hand what the most current techniques are and try to adopt them into your style and skill set.

Races offer a number of different classes that take into consideration racing experience and ability level so that newcomers are competing against newcomers and not national champions.

In all areas of a sport, recreational technique develops as a by-product of racing because of the need for competitors to have an efficient and energy conserving style. They are concerned about covering the greatest amount of distance in as short a period of time while expending as little energy as possible. This can only be done through efficiency, which is learned through repeated practice sessions and muscle memory of technique that allows you to accomplish a great deal of work with a limited output of energy and effort.

The ultimate goal is to accomplish difficult moves while making it look as easy and effortless as possible, which is only possible through technique, finesse and style. Poling is nothing more than an application of angle and leverage. What makes some of us better than others is practice in all types of conditions, which racing provides.

Competition will provide you the exposure to the fastest and easiest ways to push straight up or down a river as a result of competing in the wildwater classes, as well as developing the ability to make the canoe dance through a complex rock garden with the exactness of ballerinas on stage by entering slalom classes.

Nothing compares to the feeling of taking everything that the river can throw at you and picking apart a rock garden with spins, ferries, U turns, reverse moves, climbing drops front wards and backwards, surfing holes and waves while doing "rock hops" and "rock-a-copters" in the middle of froth and foam. So lets explore the aspects of canoe racing with a pole.

Poling competitions are divided up into two major categories and ability/age groups:

Wildwater:

The first is Wildwater which is essentially nothing more than starting at point A and racing to point B, rounding the designated turnaround point and then returning back to point A as fast as you can. In this case the competitor has to survey the course ahead of time looking for the shortest and fastest way possible.

This requires significant river reading skills and assessment for finding the channels that allow one to move forward as quickly as possible with as few correctional moves as possible. The more zigzagging caused by avoiding rocks, the slower you will be as speed is sacrificed for corrections.

Wildwater requires the highest degree of fitness possible, as it is both anaerobic requiring large muscle movements in the upper body to generate brute strength, as well as aerobic capacity with the cardiovascular system to endure the high heart rate of the sprint like race.

Wildwater courses are usually set up to last between four and six minutes for the top racers. This means the lesser skilled racers will be completing the course in six to ten minutes.

In Wildwater, you are allowed to get back into your canoe if you happen to flip or fall out. You are not allowed to advance your canoe if you are outside the hull.

Always carry at least one to two spare poles as the chance of pinning one and losing it are very high depending on the type of river bottom.

The rules require that you round the turnaround buoy(s) or you are disqualified.

Racers go off one at a time in a time trial fashion so you are racing against the clock, with the fastest time winning.

Courses can be set so that the starting point is either upstream or downstream of the single turnaround point. In some cases it can be in the middle of the course so that two turnaround buoys have to be set which forces the poler to decide whether to go downstream first or upstream.

Strategy enters into this as it depends on which leg is the most difficult and will use the most energy. Usually, the racer will try to get the most difficult leg done first while their energy levels are the highest, saving the easier section for last. Often the poler will attack the upstream section first, then rest on the downstream section in preparation for the last uphill section on the return to the starting point.

The poler is required to "horseshoe" around the turnaround buoys without having to tie the knot or cross their path of entry on the way out.

Slalom:

The second major category is Slalom which is a combination of finesse, technical ability and speed.

A slalom course is set up using buoys to define the natural moves a poler would normally utilize on the river given the features of rocks, eddies and waves.

Generally there can be anywhere from 15 to 30 buoys placed

to design a course based on the length and complexity of the rapid. A well designed course will take the top racers anywhere from four to eight minutes to complete and will have a variety of gates which use the natural features of the river to require the poler to show their ability and efficiency at negotiating the course based both on speed and technical proficiency for the fastest time possible.

Polers are given two runs with the fastest time being the official one posted in the final results.

Moves will include a combination of eddy turns, upstream and downstream poling, forward and reverse moves, circle moves, and ferries. The tighter the course, the more difficult and complex it becomes.

If a poler capsizes or falls out of the canoe, their run is over resulting in a "DNF" (did not finish) designation.

Penalty times of 10 seconds are assessed if you touch a buoy with your pole, canoe or body and 50 seconds if you fail to properly negotiate or miss a buoy. Needless to say, a clean run without penalties is required for a top place finish.

Marking out and understanding the course:

Buoys are made of empty plastic one gallon jugs with a hole cut in the top to make it easy to fill with water and to empty. They are color coded to determine what the proper move is. Empty milk or plastic detergent bottles come in the white, red and green colors you need to set a course.

Red or green tape creating offsetting contrasting horizontal stripes on the buoy will easily produce reverse jugs.

- The jugs or buoys are placed on rocks to designate the appropriate moves.
- Circle buoys are white and require the racer to tie their knot, in other words, cross their line of entry as they exit the circle within a canoe length of the rock being circled. You can go forwards or backwards around the buoy as long as you complete the loop.
- Solid colors designate forward gates and striped colors mean reverse gates. Red is always on your left and

green is always on your right.

- As an example, a solid green followed by a striped red requires the poler to pass the green (with the green on their right) moving forward, and then spin the canoe in time to require passage in reverse with the red stripe on the boaters left. This could be either done traveling upstream or downstream based on the layout of the course and what the intent of the course designer is.
- Eddy turns are signified by buoys that have split colors. The top half may be green and the bottom red or vice versa.
- Use spray paint to change the color on the top or bottom half of the buoy based on what type of eddy turn you are trying to designate. The top color signifies whether or not it is a right or left eddy turn.
- If the top is green and the bottom red, then it is a right eddy turn requiring the poler to keep the green on their right side as they enter the eddy, and then have the bottom red on their left as they exit the eddy.
- Eddy turns are not spins while moving downstream with the current. They require that the boater turn into the eddy, stopping all downstream progress before exiting the eddy. This can be a very fast maneuver with the racer using his/her momentum to carve an arc through the turn so that as little speed as possible is lost.
- The boater must pass within a canoe length of the buoy for the gate to be active and count, otherwise incurring a 50 second penalty.
- The gate becomes live once the leading end of the canoe breaks the perpendicular plane of the buoy and goes dead once the entire canoe leaves the plane of the gate.
- There is no penalty if the buoy is touched after the gate has been completed.

Slalom courses are a lot of fun and are by far the best way for measuring an individual's total proficiency as a poler in that they require both river reading skills, speed, technical ability, finesse and total control of the boat.

Competition Classes:

Slalom and Wildwater categories are further broken down into separate classes based on age and ability levels.

- Youth classes are for any racer 18 years and younger. Intermediate classes are for entry and beginner level racers.
- Once you win the intermediate class in either wildwater or slalom, you are then required to enter the open class in that respective event.
- The open class is generally for the more experienced racers including national champions. Anyone can enter the open class and you are able to win it multiple times as opposed to the intermediate class which forces you to leave the class once you win it.
- Masters classes are designated for anyone 40 years and up and can be won multiple times.
- Grand masters classes are for individuals 60 years and up and can be won multiple times.
- Because of the increasing fitness levels of older racers, it was important to provide another category for polers over 60.
- All classes are open to both sexes although female classes are possible if you have enough entries.
- A minimum of three entries is required to make up a class.

American Canoe Association:

In American Canoe Association competition, individual trophies and awards are given to the top three place finishers in any category or class. There are also permanent traveling trophies which stay with the winning individual until they lose to another competitor.

The individual's name and year of winning the trophy are engraved as a permanent record of who has won over the years of the event.

The ACA has permanent traveling bowls for Open Wildwater and Open Slalom as national individual title events.

Combination Trophies:

- There are also two combined bowls which recognize the top combined racer in both events. This requires the racer to use the same canoe in both events, thus looking for a canoe that is equally versed in the need for speed in wildwater and nimble turning ability in slalom. Points are awarded in both events and the person with the highest number of points is crowned the overall national champion.
- First place is awarded three points, second place two points and third place one point.
- In the event that two competitors have the same number of points between both events, the percentage margin difference of how much faster one racer was over the other in each event is calculated to determine who was faster overall.
- As an example, if two competitors each score a first and second place, then they both have five points. Now you must compare how much faster one racer was over the other in each respective event to determine the overall national champion.
- There are always three clocks on each racer with the high and low times being thrown out and the middle time being the official time.

Many races have been decided on hundredths of a second so accurate time keeping and scoring of penalty points is critical.

At national level events, gate judges are required to watch and ensure that slalom moves are properly executed and that there are no missed or touched buoys resulting in penalty points.

16. CONCLUSION

So grab the big stick and remember to stand tall as you make the big push upriver.

You will be greeted with a number of "insightful" remarks from floaters who are convinced you are moving in the wrong direction but pay them little heed. They are the ones who are moving in the wrong direction.

The heritage of canoe sport started with the pole before the development of the paddle and continued with the exploration and mapping of the North American continent through the Voyageurs and explorers such as Lewis and Clark. It has been used commercially for moving freight up and down rivers as well as militarily in the Revolutionary War to transport troops and supplies.

It is still used today by wilderness guides taking their "sports" or clients into the otherwise unreachable pristine waters of rivers and lakes where roadways do not exist.

Mostly, it is a wonderful and fun way of recreationally using the empty canoe in rapids and pitting our strength and abilities against the ever challenging scope of the river.

We are continuing that tradition and heritage by being head and shoulders above all those paddlers as we climb drops and eddy hop against the relentless current.

Always remember that we are the "upstanding example" of what canoe sport is all about as we stand tall and carry a big stick!

APPENDIX A. CREDITS

Photo Credits

Gail Ambrosino:
Plates; 5, 6, 7, 8, 9,10, 11, 12, 13, 15, 23.
Taken on the Connecticut River in Holyoke, Massachusetts

Anne Rock:
Front cover, Back cover and Plates; 1, 2, 3, 4, 14, 16, 17, 18, 19, 20, 21, 22.
Taken on the Farmington River in Tariffville Gorge

Illustrations by Sarah Smith

Designed and Edited by Colin Broadway

APPENDIX B. FURTHER READING

Regretfully there are few books available on the fascinating subject of canoe polin, many complete guides to canoeing offer a single paragraph on poling, even more offer nothing. Most of the titles listed below are now out of print, however at the time of publishing, Amazon.co.uk appeared to have limited stocks of most titles.

Canoeing, The American National Red Cross,
        Doubleday & Company Ltd Various editions

Pole, Paddle & Portage, Bill Riviere
        Van Nostrand Reinhold Company 1969

The Canoe Guides Handbook, Gil Gilpatrick
        DeLorme Publishing Company 1981

The Open Canoe, Bill Riviere
        Little Brown and Company, 1985

Punts and Punting, R.T.Rivington
        R.T.Rivington 1982

Beyond the Paddle, Garrett Conover, Jerry Stelmok
        Tilbury House Publishers, 1991

Canoe Poling, Al, Syl & Frank Beletz
        A.C. Mackenzie Press, 1974

The Basic Essentials of Canoe Poling, Harry Rock
        ICS Books, Inc. 1992

INDEX